Edgar Cayce's
Secrets of Astrology

Edgar Cayce's Secrets of Astrology

Planets, Signs, Aspects, and Sojourns

by Kirk Nelson

ASSOCIATION FOR
RESEARCH AND
ENLIGHTENMENT

A.R.E. Press • Virginia Beach • Virginia

A.R.E. Press
215 67th Street
Virginia Beach, VA 23451-2061

Library of Congress Cataloging-in-Publication Data
Nelson, Kirk.
Edgar Cayce's secrets of astrology : planets, signs, aspects, and sojourns / by Kirk Nelson
    p. cm.
ISBN 0-87604-420-8
1. Astrology. 2. Cayce, Edgar, 1877-1945. Edgar Cayce
readings. I. Title.
BF1711.N39   1999
133.5'092–dc21   98-45857

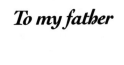

To my father

Table of Contents

Illustrations

Author's Note

I love astrology. To me it is interesting, fun, complex, and even simple, all at the same time. I have studied it for over twenty years, and I am still learning about its intricacies.

Many people are put off by astrology because they feel it is too complex. This is the great dichotomy of astrology: It can be both extremely simple and extremely complex.

Astrologers often become caught up in the minute details of astrology, saying, for example, that because a certain planet is in a certain sign, specific things will occur. But I find that astrology works best in the extremes. By that I mean that astrological effects are most easily observed when large groupings of planets are in a certain sign or arrangement. So, as an astrologer, what I try to do is look for large groupings of planets, and, using this method, I often observe some amazing results.

As an example, I can cite the experience of my two friends, Gary and Darlene. A few years ago there was a conjunction of eight planets in Capricorn. I knew that this would be a bad configuration for Darlene, who is a Libra, but a good one for Gary, who is a Pisces, and I told them so. One day, when I arrived at work, Gary came up to me and said, "You were so right. I just got a promotion to the job I have always wanted." Five minutes later Darlene walked over and said, "You were right. This has been a terrible time for me. I am getting a divorce." Both my friends had just seen tremendous changes in their lives, showing the amazing value of astrology.

But how can this be? How can planets millions of miles away have an effect upon us here on earth? The reason is that everything in the universe is connected to everything else in the universe.

Evidence for this is contained in a scientific theory by physicist J. S. Bell, known as Bell's Theorem. In a complicated series of mathematical proofs, he proved that objects in the universe are connected to every other object in the universe, even though they may be separated by great distances.

This was proven experimentally in the laboratory in the following manner: Two electrons were sent off in opposite directions. Scientists then changed the direction of one of the electrons and discovered that this affected the other electron, even though there was no apparent physical connection between them. This experiment showed that there is an extraphysical connection among objects in the universe.

Astrology is not the only influence in an individual's life, and I think astrologers sometimes tend to ignore this. There are family, hereditary, and cultural influences as well as the most important influence of all—the will of the individual and the choices he or she makes in life. So astrological influences must be considered within the context of who a person is and where he or she is in life. When I read an astrological chart, I first ask the individual to tell me about his or her life history. This is because even when two people are born at exactly the same time on the same day, the astrology will have a different meaning for each individual.

If you were to do a chart for the president of the United States and a gas station attendant born at the same time on the same day, the chart would have a different meaning for each of them, even though the planets were in the same positions.

As an example, if they had an astrological aspect in the future that would tend to make them more aggressive, because of their different positions in life the aspect would take on a different meaning for each. The gas station attendant might argue with a customer, while the president might send his troops to war. So, the most important consideration in astrology is to examine the influences within the context of the individuals involved.

If you want to study your own astrology, it is best to look at yourself and your own life first. Write down your goals and what you are doing to meet those goals. Then study the astrological aspects on a daily basis, and learn how they affect you. I guarantee that it will be a rewarding and valuable experience.

1

EDGAR CAYCE

Edgar Cayce was the greatest psychic in American history. He lived from 1877 to 1945 and gave over 14,000 readings, nearly all of which were recorded and are still preserved today. Two-thirds of Cayce's readings were devoted to healing the sick. He would lie on his couch, go into a trancelike state, and, after being given only the name and address of the sick person, would give an accurate diagnosis, including the appropriate remedies. The balance of the readings covered a variety of other topics. His abilities were so profound that his fame put him on the front page of the magazine section of the *New York Times* on October 9, 1910.

The followers of Edgar Cayce formed an organization, the Association for Research and Enlightenment, Inc., to study and research his psychic readings. The A.R.E., with its headquarters in Virginia Beach, Virginia, now boasts a membership of over 20,000. It houses a large library, bookstore, and the records of Cayce's readings.

It is helpful for people who want to learn about Cayce's readings to understand the source of the information that came through him. Fortunately, we have an explanation from Edgar Cayce himself, delivered in a speech on February 6, 1933:

It is rather hard to describe something which has become so much a part of me. It is almost like trying to describe what my face looks like— I can show you, but I can't tell you. I can tell you some of my experiences and my thoughts in respect to the readings; but as to what a reading is—well, I can only tell you what other people have said about them and the thoughts that have come to me as I have studied effects created in the minds of those who have received the readings.

It wouldn't be an exaggeration to say that I have been in the unconscious state, during which the readings are given, perhaps 25,000 times during the last thirty-one years. Yet I myself have never heard a single reading! Then how can I describe one to you?

Many people who have never heard a reading have asked me how I knew I could give one. I never did know it—and don't know it yet—except by taking another person's word for it!

The first step in giving a reading is this: I loosen my clothes—shoelaces, necktie, shirtcuffs, belt—so that I have a perfectly free-flowing circulation. Next, I lie down on the couch in my office. If the reading is to be a "physical" one, I lie with my head to the south; if it is to be a "life" reading, my head is to the north, and feet to south. I myself do not know the reason for this difference in polarization, as the readings themselves called it.

When I am lying comfortably, I put both my

hands up to my forehead—to the spot where others have told me that the third eye is located—and I pray. Interestingly enough, it seems that I have instinctively and unconsciously, from the very beginning, adopted the practices used by initiates in meditation. Putting the hands upon the point on the forehead midway between the two eyes is an example of what I mean.

After praying, I wait for a few minutes until I receive what might be called the "go" signal—that is, a flash of brilliant white light, sometimes verging upon a golden color. The light is a sign to me that I have made contact. Until I have seen it, I know that I cannot give the reading.

After I have seen this light, I move both my hands down to the solar plexus. Then, I'm told, my breathing becomes very deep and rhythmic, from the diaphragm. Several minutes go by. When my eyelids begin to flutter closed—having been open but glazed thus far—the conductor knows I am ready to receive the suggestion. He proceeds to give it to me, slowly and distinctly. For example, if it is a physical reading, the name of the person and the address where he may be located at that time are given to me. Then there is a pause—sometimes so long a pause, I'm told, that I appear not to have heard the directions. If so, they are given to me again; and after that, I repeat the name and address very slowly, until the body is located and a description of its condition is begun.

This, then, is how I give a reading. I am entirely unconscious during the whole procedure. When I wake up, I feel as if I had slept a little bit too long. Frequently I feel slightly hungry; just hungry enough, perhaps, for a cracker and a glass of milk.

As to the validity of the information which comes through me when I sleep: this is the question, naturally, that occurs to everyone. Personally, I feel that its validity depends largely upon how much faith and confidence lie within the one who seeks this source of information. Its validity, of course, has been objectively proved many hundreds of times, by the results that have come from applying the advice obtained.

In regard to the source of information, naturally I have some ideas about it. But even though I have been doing this work for thirty-one years, I know very little about it. Whatever I might say would be largely a matter of conjecture. I can make no claims whatsoever to great knowledge, for I also am only groping.

But then, we all learn by experience, do we not? We come to have faith and understanding only by taking one step at a time. Most of us don't have the experience of getting religion all at once—like the man who got it halfway between the bottom of the well and the top, when he was blown out by an explosion of dynamite. Most of us need to have experiences and to arrive at conclusions by weighing the evidence along with something that answers from deep within our inner selves.

As a matter of fact, there would seem to be not just one, but several sources of information tapped when I am in this sleeping state. One source, apparently, is the record made by an individual, or entity, in all of its experiences through what we call time. The sum total of the experiences of that soul is written, so to speak, in the subconscious of that individual as well as in what is known as the Akashic records. Anyone may read these records, if he can attune himself rightly. Apparently, I am one of the few people who may lay aside the personality sufficiently to allow the soul to make this attunement to the universal source of knowledge. I say this, however, not in a boastful way; in fact, I don't claim to possess any power that any other person doesn't possess. I sincerely believe that there isn't any person, anywhere, who doesn't have the same ability I have. I'm certain that all human beings have much greater powers than they are ever aware of—providing they are willing to pay the price of detachment from self-interest which is required to develop those powers or abilities. Would you be willing, even once a year, to put aside your own personality—to pass entirely away from it?

Now, some people think that the information coming through me is given by some departed personality who wishes to communicate: some benevolent spirit or guide from the other side. This may sometimes be true, but in general I am not a "medium" in that sense of the term. If the person who seeks a reading, however, comes seeking that kind of contact and information, I believe he receives that kind.

Many people ask me how I prevent undesirable influences from entering into the work I do. In order to answer that question, let me tell an experience I had when I was a child. When I was between eleven and twelve years of age, I had read the Bible through, three times. Now I have read it fifty-six times. No doubt some people have read it more times than that; but I have tried to read it once for each year of my life.

Well, as a child, I prayed that I might be able to do something for other people—to aid them in understanding themselves, and especially to aid children in their ills. One day I had a vision which convinced me that my prayer had been heard and would be answered.

So I believe that my prayer is being answered; and as I go into the unconscious condition, I do so with that faith. I also believe that the source of information will be from the Universal, if the connection is not made to waver, by the desires of the person seeking the reading.

Of course, if that person's desire is very intense to have a communication from Grandpa, Uncle, or some great soul; then the contact is directed that way and such becomes the source.

Do not think I am discrediting those who seek in such a way. If you're willing to receive what Uncle Joe has to say, that is what you get. If you're willing to depend upon a more Universal Source, then that is what you get.

"What ye ask, ye shall receive" is like a two-edged sword. It cuts both ways.

Edgar Cayce was able to roll back his physical consciousness, go through the subconscious, and connect with his superconscious—that part of all of us that is linked with the Universal Consciousness, or God. This ability of Cayce's is what gives his readings such great power.

While most of Cayce's readings were physical or philosophical in nature, he also gave approximately 2,000 life readings, which involve reincarnation, personal and business problems, and sometimes astrology. The readings in which Cayce gave astrological information are the ones that are of interest to us here.

2

CAYCE'S VIEW OF ASTROLOGY

Edgar Cayce's view of astrology is based on the concept of reincarnation. He felt that it was not the positions of the planets that influence the soul at birth, but that the soul chooses the time in which it wishes to be born. Most of us, according to Cayce, have had lives before this one, and we bring with us talents, abilities, and influences from those past lives. These influences, part of the Law of Cause and Effect, are called "karma" in Sanskrit.

Cayce also tells us that not only have we had previous lives, but that the soul has a life outside the physical world between lifetimes. During these interim periods, the soul experiences levels of consciousness that correspond to the vibratory levels of the different planets. Cayce referred to these interim lifetime experiences as "planetary sojourns."

Because we have had experiences with the vibrations of the different planets between lifetimes, the planets have an internal influence on us when we reincarnate into the earth plane. These influences of the planets are felt by us in the form of "urges, inclinations, and tendencies." However, Cayce says, no influence is greater than the human will and the choices we make in our lives every day. Several readings* provide us with details on Cayce's view:

> Astronomy is considered a science and astrology as foolishness. Who is correct? One holds that because of the position of the earth, the sun, the planets, they are balanced one with another in some manner, some form; yet that they have nothing to do with man's life or the expanse of life, or the emotions of the physical being in the earth.
>
> Then, why and how do the effects of the sun *so* influence other life in the earth and not affect *man's* life, man's emotions?
>
> As the sun has been set as the ruler of this solar system, does it not appear to be reasonable that it *has* an effect upon the inhabitants of the earth, as well as upon plant and mineral life in the earth?
>
> Then if not, why, how did the ancients worship the sun *as* the representative of a continuous benevolent and beneficent influence upon the life of the individual?
>
> Thus as we find given, the sun and the moon and the stars were made also—this being the attempt of the writer to convey to the individual the realization that there *is* an influence in their activity! For, remember, they—the sun, the

---

*Each reading is indexed by two sets of numbers. The first set identifies the person or group for whom the reading was given ("281"); the second set refers to the number in the series ("-2").

moon, the planets—have their marching orders from the divine, and they move in same.

Man alone is given that birthright of free will. He alone may defy his God! 5757-1

We are all cocreators with God, and our free will is the birthright that makes us creators. As such, in our world and in our lives, we have the choice to create good or evil.

Q. Do the planets have anything to do with the ruling of the destiny of men? If so, what? and what do they have to do with this body?

A. They do. In the beginning, as our own planet, Earth, was set in motion, the placing of other planets began the ruling of the destiny of all matter as created, just as the division of waters was and is ruled by the moon in its path about the Earth; just so as in the higher creation, as it began, is ruled by the action of the planets about the earth.

The strongest power in the destiny of man is the Sun, first; then the closer planets, or those that are coming in ascendancy at the time of the birth of the individual; but let it be understood here, no action of any planet or any of the phases of the Sun, Moon, or any of the heavenly bodies surpass the rule of Man's individual will power— the power given by the Creator of man in the beginning, when he became a living soul, with the power of choosing for himself.

The inclination of man is ruled by the planets under which he is born. In this far the destiny of man lies within the sphere or scope of the planets. With the given position of the Solar system at the time of the birth of an individual, it can be worked out—that is, the inclinations and actions

without the will power taken into consideration.
254-2

Astrology is a fact, in most instances. But as-
trological aspects are but signs, symbols. *No in-*
***fluence* is of greater value or of greater help than**
the *will* of an individual.   815-6

Cayce's belief in human self-reliance goes so far as to
say that the stars don't rule us, we rule the stars!

These influences are not greater than the will
of the entity. While the varied aspects may be
said to *rule* the entity, yet the *entity*—as every-
one—should rather, with its own will, *rule* those
integral aspects in the affairs—of the stars, as
well as of self's own life. Rather, then, than the
stars *ruling* the life, the life should rule the
stars—for man was created a little bit higher than
all the rest of the whole universe, and is capable
of harnessing, directing, enforcing, the laws of
the universe.   5-2

In his readings Cayce describes human beings as
cocreators with God. This means that God created us
for companionship and endowed us with free will and
the ability to create. It is this ability that makes us Godlike, for the Bible says that God created humans in His
own image. Here are some readings in which Cayce
shows our relationship to God and to astrology:

As indicated in the certain periods, remem-
ber—as has been given—it is not because ye were
born in May, or on the 4th of May, that such and
such happened to thee. For, as a corpuscle in the
body of God, ye are free-willed—and thus a co-
creator with God.   3003-1

In all influences, as are seen, that are as stan-
dards or as signposts along life's way, these are

written—as it were—in the astrological influences that have influenced and do influence an entity through any given experience or time; yet, as has oft been given, there is no influence in the experience of an entity that does surpass the will, or the ability to act or react as is the gift of every individual that is a child of the Creative Forces, or God; for that is which makes an entity, a soul, Godlike—the ability to choose or to *will* that which its attributes or its mind or body may be used in this or that expression of the attributes of that it worships.   288-30

Cayce is clear that the application of free will involves choice, and the most important aspect of choice is what we choose as our ideal.

While the period of the year, the place of birth, the environs through the developing of an entity in any one appearance, the numerological conditions and names have their influence, *none* of these equal or surpass that which an entity does concerning that it *knows* as in relation to that it sets as its ideal!   353-1

Hence the influences of choice may surpass even the experiences that have been a part of the entity through any astrological or earthly-material sojourn.   2462-2

Urges, Inclinations, and Tendencies

As previously mentioned, Cayce often described the influences of the planets in our lives in terms of "urges, inclinations, and tendencies." This means that astrological influences are an internal influence within our minds, rather than an external influence coming from outside of ourselves.

As an example, Venus represents love in the zodiac,

and if a person has a strong Venus aspect at a particular time, he or she might feel more loving. This in turn would attract the love of others to that person. But the astrological influence would start as an internal feeling that became manifested outwardly due to what Cayce would call a "mental urge."

Because the human will is superior to any mental urge, it is up to us to choose which inclinations we follow and which ones we resist, thereby exercising our moral judgment. The following readings further explain Cayce's view:

Q. Is it proper for us to study the effects of the planets on our lives in order to better understand our tendencies and inclinations, as influenced by the planets?

A. When studied aright, very, very, very much so. How aright then? In that influence as is seen in the influence of the knowledge already obtained by mortal man. Give more of that into the lives, giving the understanding *that the will must be the ever guiding factor to lead man on, ever upward.*   3744-4

Astrological aspects may or may not become a part of the experience physically for the entity. For these are merely urges, and the will—that which designates God's creation of man from the rest of the animal world—rules as to what an individual soul does with opportunities in relationships with the fellow man.   3340-1

It is true, then, that there are latent and manifested urges, manifested abilities, manifested virtues, manifested faults, in the experience of each entity. These faults, these virtues may be pointed out, yet the usage, the application of same is of free will—that which is the universal gift to the

**souls of the children of men; that each entity may
know itself to be itself and yet one with the universal cause.   2620-2**

Another example of how these urges, inclinations,
and tendencies manifest in the physical world is pro-
vided in the following reading:

**But as the body physically comes under the in-
clination or tendencies of affectation from astrological influences, and there is the tendency for
the mental self to dwell upon same, it lends itself
then—unless resistances are builded in the mental and physical reactions—towards those tendencies or inclinations that arise.**

**Such conditions are oft in the experience of
individuals termed or classified as accidents.**

470-14

What Cayce is telling us in this reading is that if a
person comes under an adverse astrological aspect (angular relationship between planets; see page 96), it can
actually lead to a physical accident. I have seen this in
my own life with a strong correlation between bad Mars
aspects and sports injuries.

Almost every time I have had a severe sports injury, I
have been under a bad Mars influence. The way this
works is that bad Mars aspects tend to make you more
aggressive, because Mars is the planet of violence and
aggression. The more aggressive you are, the more
likely you are to overextend or rush what you are doing
and have an accident or an injury. It is this mental attitude of overaggression that leads to accidents.

Whenever I have sustained serious sports injuries,
Mars had been in a bad relationship with the Sun that
day. It got to be such a pattern that I became aware of it
and began to tone down my actions during those time
periods to prevent any more such injuries.

After I discovered this relationship, I had an interesting experience with one of my astrology clients. I did a chart for a teenage girl who had a predominately positive chart. Her mother wanted to know, however, why the girl was always having accidents around the house, breaking things, or cutting herself. I looked at her birth chart (the horoscope or map of the heavens at the time of her birth) and discovered that she had a bad Mars-Sun relationship. When I asked her mother if she had a tendency to rush when she was doing things at home, her mother replied, "Yes, definitely." I told her that this aggressive attitude was reflected in the bad Mars aspect and that she just needed to slow down.

This story is a good illustration of the value of astrology. The birth chart revealed a personality tendency that needed to be changed. Now that the girl is aware of it, she can use her will to change in a positive direction.

Planetary Sojourns

One astrological concept that is unique to the Cayce readings is the idea of "planetary sojourns." Cayce tells us that every soul between lifetimes experiences a consciousness that corresponds to the vibrations of the various planets. These "trips" to the levels of vibration of the various planets, not physical incarnations, are called planetary sojourns. They occur between lifetimes and are the basis for astrological influences.

Q. Would it be well for me to make a study of astrology?

A. Well for everyone to make a study of astrology! for, as indicated, while many individuals have set about to prove the astrological aspects and astrological survey enable one to determine future as well as the past conditions, these are

well to the point where the individual under-
stands that these act upon individuals because of
their sojourn or correlation of their associations
with the environs through which these are
shown—see? Rather than the star directing the
life, the life of the individual directs the courses
of the stars, see . . .   311-10

Then there are the sojourns in other realms of
the solar system which represent certain attributes. Not that ye maintain a physical earth-
body in Mercury, Venus, Jupiter, Uranus or
Saturn; but there is an awareness or a consciousness in those realms when absent from the body,
and the response to the position those planets
occupy in this solar system . . .

So, all of those realms—as in Mercury, Venus,
Jupiter, Saturn, Uranus—have their realms of
consciousness also.   2823-1

The soul experiences an awareness or a consciousness of the various planetary realms when absent from
the body, according to Cayce. This is not a physical
awareness, but an experience in the soul's consciousness.

In giving the interpretations we find those influences as might be termed by some astrological, though from here we view them rather as
experiences of the entity's consciousness through
that realm. To give it metes and bounds we call it
the names indicated by astrological aspects—
Mercury, Venus, Jupiter, Neptune and Uranus;
with Saturn in between.   2995-1

Venus, Mercury, Uranus and Neptune are the
greater influence from the astrological sojourns;
not because these appear so prominently in what
would be called the chart of the entity, owing to
its birth, but because of the entity's indwelling

**and activities through those sojourns there is the
interims between the material sojourns. 2073-2**

Cayce refers to the movement from these planetary
experiences between lives to birth in the earth plane as
the soul "taking flight." If the last planet visited by the
soul's consciousness had been Venus, Cayce would say
that "the soul took its flight from Venus."

Q. Explain how, why, and in what manner, planets influence an individual at birth?

**A. As the entity is born into the earth's plane,
the relation to that planet, or that sphere, from
which the spirit entity took its flight, or its position, to enter the earth plane, has the greater influence in the earth's plane. Just as the life lived
in the earth's plane directs to what position the
spirit entity takes in the sphere.   900-24**

The planet from which a soul took its flight is the
planet that has the greatest influence on a person's life,
just as the family we are born into has the greatest influence on our life once we are in the earth plane.

The experience of planetary sojourns is that of digesting or assimilating the experiences we have had in
the previous lifetime. If you think of the earth as a
school, as Cayce suggests, then there are lessons to be
learned here.

Planetary sojourns can be likened to an introspective
period between school days. One day you learn something in school, think about it after school, and the next
day you learn something else. Every lifetime we learn
soul lessons, and in between lifetimes, during our planetary sojourns, we absorb, digest, and assimilate the lessons of the previous lifetime. Then we reincarnate to
learn more lessons until we achieve perfection.

The following readings show how Cayce described

some of these sojourns and the roles they play in our lives:

> The shadows of those things from the sojourns
> of this entity in Mercury, Jupiter, Saturn, Ura-
> nus, Venus and the influences of the general
> system's activity as in the Sun and Moon, have
> their portion in the very relationships and activ-
> ity of the entity. These are but the mental urges
> that arise, and become as the individuality of an
> entity in expression in the material world; while
> the appearances in the earth through the various
> sojourns that are become active in the experience
> of an entity at any one given place or position or
> appearance or period, are as but the personality
> in the entity's experience—and are as the urges
> from the emotions that have been created.
>
> Just as the entity's attending this or that uni-
> versity, this or that place of learning, would make
> for a parlance peculiar unto itself. Even though
> individuals may study the same line of thought,
> one attending Harvard, another Yale, another
> Oxford, another Stanford, another the university
> of Arizona, they each would carry with them the
> vibrations created by their very activity in those
> environs.   633-2

We all carry with us the influence of our past experiences, and planetary sojourns are experiences that we
all have had. Therefore, they have a similar influence
on us as a particular school, family, or homeland.

> As we find, those that may be the more help-
> ful, applicable and practical in the present expe-
> rience, would be—we would direct—from the
> astrological sojourns, rather than from other in-
> clinations; for these, as we find, deal more di-
> rectly with the mental and material inclinations
> of an entity in most appearances in the earth.

> For, as seen from a sojourn in an environment
> that is in the experience of this entity, in that of
> Jupiter; these influences deal more directly with
> impulses, inclination, trend of thought, and that
> which produces same. It is much as the manner
> of dwelling in a particular clime or country influ-
> ences an entity, as the entity experiences from
> the Fatherland and the adopted land.
>
> Hence, as the customs or the laws of varied
> experiences or sojourns wield that trend of
> thought in an individual's experience in earth's
> sojourn, so does the environ to the soul and its
> soul body affect impulses in an entity's activities
> in a material sojourn.   373-2

These prebirth sojourns operate in our lives because
when death occurs in the physical, the soul experiences
a birth into the spiritual. Once absent from the body,
the soul is, in fact, in the presence of God. This new life
in the spiritual realm then takes in the qualities of the
various planets in which the soul sojourns.

> Then, a death in the flesh is a birth into the
> realm of another experience, to those who have
> lived in such a manner as not to be bound by
> earthly ties. This does not mean that it does not
> have its own experience about the earth, but that
> it has lived such a *fullness* of life that it must be
> about its business.   989-2
>
> Just as when there are those various realms about
> the solar system in which each entity may find
> itself when absent from the body, it takes on in
> those other realms not an earthly form but a pat-
> tern—conforming to the same dimensional ele-
> ments of that individual planet or space. 2533-8

According to Cayce, each planetary realm has a different number of dimensions—more than the three we

experience in the physical plane on earth.

Astrological aspects—not because the stars were in such a position, but because of the activities of the entity as an entity through that consciousness accredited to the various phases or dimensions of activity—we find in the earth plane the three dimensions, in Venus the four, in Jupiter the five, in Uranus the seven—all of these; not as of planes, as sometimes spoken of, but consciousnesses—the ability to reason from certain activities.   3006-1

According to Cayce, the planetary realms can actually have as many as eight dimensions.

The souls that are aware of their being in a consciousness as they pass through the environ, or the dimension of that consciousness. Just as in the earth it is known as three dimensions, yet man may think in an eight-dimensional consciousness.   3037-1

This eight-dimensional consciousness may be related to what is known as the Law of Octaves. In music you count seven notes before moving to a new octave: do, re, mi, fa, so, la, ti, do. In the human body you must move up through the seven endocrine centers to reach a higher level.

The Law of Octaves is also demonstrated in nature by the fact that the genetic code, which transmits hereditary traits to offspring, contains 64 (8x8) bits of information. Humankind includes it in its own systems in the 64 elements of the *I Ching*, 64 squares on a chess board, and by the arrangement of all computers on a base 16 (2x8) system.

It is also possible that this eight-dimensional consciousness is something that we who are living in three-dimensional consciousness cannot understand. The example of the two-dimensional flatlander is often used: If you were a two-dimensional person you would be aware only of a two-dimensional reality, like a flat piece of paper. If a dot on the piece of paper were picked up and moved to another part of the paper by a three-dimensional being, it would appear to the two-dimensional person that the dot had disappeared from one place and reappeared in another because a two-dimensional being would not be aware of the dot's movement through the third dimension. Likewise, it may be just as hard for us as three-dimensional beings to be aware of realities in other dimensions.

So, while we do not comprehend or remember the experience, when the soul passes through the planetary realms it nevertheless takes on the dimensional states of the various planets.

> **Then, as to the astrological sojourns, these are where the soul-entity is out of the material body and present with spiritual forces, that are only of a higher vibration yet are of the same materials of which matter is brought into experience as the soul enters or possesses a body in a material world; yet each experience, each phase, each realm, is that ye may become more and more consciously aware of being *in* Him, abiding in that divine creative force that only is that which is manifested in thine material surroundings as harmony, color, sound, movement, those powerful forces that are the basis of all that is good, lovely, precious in the eyes and in the whole of Him that would have thee one with Him.**

> **And the indwellings in those environs about the earth, whether—as this entity—in Venus, Jupiter, Saturn, Uranus, or in the Moon with its**

shadows of the Sun itself, these make for the expressions of the spiritual-creative influences that
are just above the matter phase, or—as a name—
in a fourth dimensional plane of activity.   818-1

After the experience in the different dimensions of
the planets, the soul enters the body at the time of birth
or shortly thereafter.

*Q. What was the exact time of entity's birth in the
present incarnation?*

A. This—the period of the *birth* and the period of the entity, or *soul* birth—is not *always* the
same. As *we* find, in the evening.

*Q. What makes the difference between the physi-
cal birth and the soul birth?*

A. One is earthy, the other is truth—or spiritual. Not that the spirit isn't—for Life is of the
Creator! That which is *given to* be the Creator's
activity enters in, even as "He breathed into him
the *breath* of life and he became a living soul."
                                                         282-3

Q. Does a soul ever enter a body before it is born?

A. It enters either at the first breath physically
drawn, or during the first twenty-four hours of
cycle activity in a material plane. Not always at
the first breath; sometimes there are hours, and
there are changes even of personalities as to the
seeking to enter.

*Q. What keeps the physical body living until the
soul enters?*

A. Spirit! For, the spirit of matter—its source
is life, or God, see?   2390-2

*Q. Should an astrological horoscope be based on
the time of physical birth or the time of soul birth?*

A. On time of physical birth; for these are merely *inclinations*, and because of inclinations are not the influence of will. *Will* is that factor of the spiritual forces or the gift, as it were, *to* man, hu-man, as he came into material form, with which choice is made, see? Hence if astrological aspects are to be assumed, then physical. But these make for oft confusing experiences to those casting such charts and reading from that which has been the version of same.   826-8

The readings tell us that souls also sojourn in other solar systems. After a soul is born into materiality in this solar system, it becomes subject to the laws of this system and must finish the cycle in this system before moving on to others.

For each soul in its advent into this earth solar system, and becoming an indweller in the realm of materiality, becomes subject to the laws and the attributes of this present solar system, with the influences from the sun, from the sun's planetary companions in this present solar experience.   510-1

Q. . . . Is it necessary to finish the solar system cycle before going to other systems?

A. Necessary to finish the solar cycle.
5749-14

When entering this system, a soul is trapped in matter until it achieves perfection in this system. Only then can it move on to other systems. This is the whole purpose of reincarnation, to keep coming back and learn lessons until the soul is totally aware, in the physical, of its relationship to God.

This potential entails what I consider to be the most beautiful philosophy in the Edgar Cayce readings: Each

of us has within our soul the pattern of the Christ Consciousness, the total awareness of our relationship with
our Creator that we can all achieve. All people on the
planet, regardless of their religion, have this awareness
within them, and it is only waiting to be awakened by
the will.

This is the purpose of reincarnation and astrological
influences: to help souls trapped in matter in this solar
system learn and evolve to the level of Spirit or God.

The Cayce readings tell us that this evolution involves our planetary sojourns between lives and that
these experiences are manifested in urges, inclinations,
and tendencies during our lives here on earth. Next we
are going to examine how these influences are reflected
in the birth chart.

3

THE SIGNS

This chapter briefly outlines the traditional view of astrology and compares it to that of the Edgar Cayce readings. The chief instrument used by astrologers is the horoscope, a map of the planetary positions at the exact time and place of a person's birth. (See Chart No. 1.) Astrologers project this map onto a circle, which they then divide into twelve equal pie-shaped sections of 30° each. These twelve sections are called the signs of the zodiac. The twelve signs are: Aries, Taurus, Gemini, Cancer, Leo, Virgo, Libra, Scorpio, Sagittarius, Capricorn, Aquarius, and Pisces. The position of the Sun at the time of a person's birth determines his or her "Sun sign."

The zodiac most commonly used in astrology is the tropical zodiac, which is determined by the position of the Sun on March 21 of each year. This is the date of the spring equinox in the Northern Hemisphere. It is the day when the Sun's rays shine directly on the equator at noon. In astrology this moment is marked as 0°

The Twelve Signs
of the Zodiac

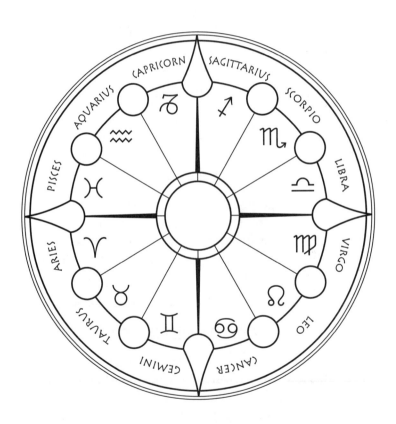

Chart No. 1

Aries and is considered the beginning of the zodiac for that year. It takes the Sun a year to move through all twelve signs of the zodiac and return to that position to begin the cycle again.

The approximate dates for the beginnings and endings of the various Sun signs are listed below:

Aries	March 21-April 19
Taurus	April 20-May 20
Gemini	May 21-June 21
Cancer	June 22-July 22
Leo	July 23-August 22
Virgo	August 23-September 22
Libra	September 23-October 23
Scorpio	October 24-November 21
Sagittarius	November 22-December 21
Capricorn	December 22-January 19
Aquarius	January 20-February 18
Pisces	February 19-March 20

The dividing point between two signs is called the cusp. If you were born on the cusp of two signs it will require an exact computation of your astrological chart to determine which sign you are. People on this dividing line are often said to have the characteristics of both signs.

The Triplicities

The signs of the zodiac are arranged in different groupings known as triplicities. (See Chart No. 2.) Four different groups of three signs display similar characteristics. These four groups are: earth signs, fire signs, water signs, and air signs.

The three earth signs are Taurus, Virgo, and Capricorn. They are considered the most practical, down-to-

The Triplicities

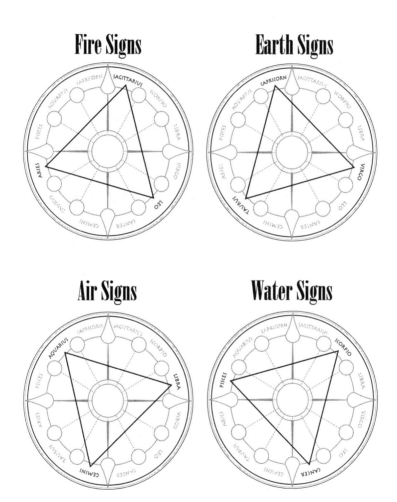

Fire Signs

Earth Signs

Air Signs

Water Signs

Chart No. 2

earth signs of the zodiac. People with the Sun in these signs tend to be good at managing money and material resources.

Taurus is the banker's sign concerned with acquiring wealth. Virgo is the sign of the meticulous and methodical technician. Capricorn is the sign of the businessperson, one who is capable of managing large-scale business endeavors.

The three fire signs are Aries, Leo, and Sagittarius. Fire-sign people are dramatic and fiery in their self-expression, ready to jump out front and lead. In Aries, this manifests in the desire to be the first in line. In Leo, it is the desire to be the center of attention. In Sagittarius, it is the more spiritual expression in philosophy, religion, or the law.

The three water signs are Cancer, Scorpio, and Pisces. Water people are concerned primarily with emotions and feelings. These are the signs of the zodiac with the deepest feelings. Cancer is a sign concerned with the home and family. In Scorpio, there is an intensity of feeling about everything in life. In Pisces, there is a sensitivity and intuitive awareness of the emotional tenor of things.

The three air signs are Aquarius, Gemini, and Libra. They deal with relationships, communication, and the intellect. Aquarius involves the universal approach to things, Gemini is the quick wit, and Libra rules relationships.

The Quadruplicities

The quadruplicities are groupings of four signs of similar characteristics. They concern methods of approach and activity in dealing with the affairs of life. The three quadruplicities are: fixed, cardinal, and mutable. (See Chart No. 3.)

The four fixed signs are Taurus, Leo, Scorpio, and Aquarius.

Their method of operation is one of fixed determination. Once these signs lock on to something they do not let go. This is good when in pursuit of a positive goal, but in the negative, it can make them rigid or stubborn. These people are consistent and determined in whatever they do.

The four cardinal signs are Aries, Cancer, Libra, and Capricorn. People with the Sun in these signs have the ability to act directly and decisively on present circumstances. They are good at sizing up immediate concerns and acting accordingly. On the positive side, this allows them to start new projects, but on the negative side, it can lead to hyperactivity and confusion.

The four mutable signs are Gemini, Virgo, Sagittarius, and Pisces. They manifest in flexibility and the ability to change in order to adjust to new conditions. People with the Sun in these signs have adaptability on the positive side, but, on the negative side, they can have a tendency to spread themselves too thin.

The Sun Signs

Each of the twelve signs of the zodiac is considered to have distinct qualities and influences in your life, the most important of which being your Sun sign. This is so important, in fact, that Cayce went so far as to say that if a person were born on the same day of the year in different lifetimes, the astrological influences would be much the same in each one.

For, as we find in this particular entity, and oft—ones that enter an experience as a complete cycle; that is, upon the same period under the

The Quadruplicities

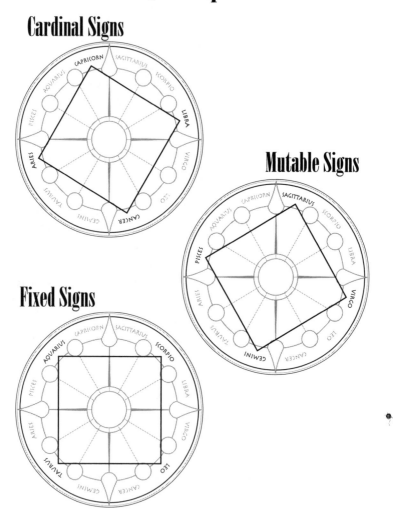

Chart No. 3

same astrological experiences as in the sojourn
just before (that is, being born upon the same
day of month—though time may have been al-
tered); find periods of activity that will be very
much the same as those manifested in the previous sojourn, in the unfoldment and in the urges
latent and manifested.   **2814-1**

The following is a brief overview of the signs with
both the traditional astrological view and Cayce's view
of the signs' influences. (Please note that some of the
explanations of Sun-sign influences will not provide
quotes from the Cayce readings because the influences
of certain signs were rarely mentioned by Cayce.)

♈ Aries
Fire Sign
Cardinal Sign
Symbol: The Ram

Aries is the first sign of the zodiac and the motto of
Aries is "Me, first." Arians like to be out front and in
the lead in everything. They are impatient—wanting
things to be done right now!

Arians make excellent leaders because of their tendency to initiate projects, but the details and the fol-
low-up are sometimes lacking. This comes from their
short attention span, which makes them want to get on
to the next activity.

With the ram as their symbol, the strength in Aries
people is in their ability to get things done, but they
must be careful not to be overly aggressive. Their anger
does not last long because of their rapidly changing natures. They can be mad as hornets one day and totally
forget about it the next.

Aries people are fiery and dramatic in their self-expression and therefore make great actors. They have a powerful presence but must be careful not to burn themselves out, as Arian stamina is not as great as some signs.

There is a story that illustrates the beauty of Aries. Two boys were given the task of cleaning two different stables of horse manure. After an hour or so the stable boss checked on one boy who was quietly cleaning. When he checked on the other boy, he found him throwing manure against the wall, on the ceiling, all over the place. When his surprised boss asked him what he was doing, he said, "I know there's a horse in here somewhere!" That is the greatness of Aries—the ability to get in there and stir things up.

In the physical body, Aries rules the head, and this is shown very clearly in Cayce's view of the influence of Aries. In fact Cayce's view of Aries is very close to the traditional astrological interpretation of Aries's influence.

> **In Aries [and Uranus] makes for those of tendencies of being easily influenced by suggestion, yet often termed by associates as very hardheaded and set in ways.   279-4**

> **In Aries—an entity that uses the head and the mental abilities, rather than the brawn or physical exertions, to accomplish that as would bring those returns for self in any material affairs. Naturally, the mental is builded likewise. 426-2**

> **As is generally termed, while the entity under Aries makes for one headstrong, head-willed, not always in the present experience has the entity applied in the sojourn that known respecting the laws of the universality of constructive or God force in its experience.   517-1**

> **One, as in Aries, that has a mind of his own, and expresses same at times to where some**

would call the entity tending towards hard-headed, or a man of his own mind.   2124-3

The following reading fits well with traditional astrology, since Aries governs the head and is ruled by the planet Mars. As we saw earlier, Mars is associated with injuries when in negative aspect.

Through Aries associations, there are the abilities of a high *mental* development; yet there are rather those warnings for this entity regarding accidents to the head. Injuries of some nature may come in the experience of the entity, either during the next four months or early portion of '34. These warnings are from influences that come from Aries or head associations with Mars.   406-1

♉ **Taurus**
    Earth Sign
    Fixed Sign
    Symbol: The Bull

Taurus is a positive, purposeful, if somewhat conservative sign of the zodiac. As an earth sign, Taurus is very concerned with the acquisition of material things. This is done in a slow, deliberate manner by focusing on a goal and working steadily toward that goal. The difference between Aries and Taurus is best illustrated by the story of the tortoise and the hare. The Taurus tortoise wins the race by being slow and steady, while the Aries hare works in bursts of energy.

Taurus is a fixed sign that may be slow to change, but once Taureans get their mind on something it is almost impossible to stop them from pursuing it with dogged determination. The Taurus symbol is the bull, and this illustrates both the strength of the sign and its earthiness.

The sign of Taurus is ruled by Venus, so its earthy nature is balanced by an appreciation of beauty. In an artistic sense, Taurus is more of a sculptor than a painter: someone who takes solid rock and carves it into something beautiful.

Taureans are very concerned with financial security and holding on to what they have and building on it. They make loyal and dedicated friends, although it may take a while to win them over.

On the positive side, their strong will drives them toward success, but on the negative side, sometimes they can be too conservative for their own good.

♊ Gemini
Air Sign
Mutable Sign
Symbol: The Twins

Gemini is the sign of the zodiac associated with intellect and communication. Geminis are communicators and do well in jobs relating to writing, speaking, or the electronic media. They can be brilliant, charming, and witty, but they need to be careful not to be too superficial. Looking into the deeper mysteries of life is not their natural bent, but it would serve them well to do so.

Gemini is an air sign, and its nature can be exemplified by the light breezes of summer. They make great conversationalists who are able to communicate with people of all walks of life in any situation.

Mercury is the ruler of Gemini, so intellectual things are very important to them. To take full advantage of this natural curiosity, early education is very important for Gemini children.

The symbol for Gemini, twins, is a perfect example

of their character. They like to have several things going on at once and are not held by conventional
thought. Gemini rules travel, so visiting other places is
important to those born under this sign. Even if they
don't travel physically, they will do a lot of mental wan-
dering.

A phrase that Edgar Cayce uses to describe the influence of Gemini is "double-mindedness." This fits perfectly with traditional astrology and the symbol of
Gemini, twins. Geminis are often of two minds, and
they must bring them together and focus to achieve success.

> For while in Gemini children there are those
> influences that make for the double-mindedness,
> in this entity it finds expression in its inclinations
> at times to change and to become speculative.
> And this has had to be curbed in the experience
> of the entity.
>
> Yet the entity would do well in any of those
> environs where there is the speculative influence.
> For the entity is, as might be termed, a favored
> one through those experiences in the earth and
> the astrological influences.   962-1
>
> In the astrological aspects, we find these as
> rather confusing. Naturally, coming under those
> signs as well as the expressions in the material
> plane of the double sign, or Gemini, there are
> two natures within the urges of the entity. One is
> to seek to know; that may oft be upon very ques-
> tionable things or conditions, even in the experi-
> ence of the entity. The other is the innate and
> manifested spiritual seeking for a greater, better,
> more perfect relationship. And these as may be
> seen in the experience are more combative one
> with another in the experience of the entity than

**as may ordinarily be experienced. Yet these be-
come, then, rather choices that are to be made in
the experience of the entity.**   **674-3**

♋ **Cancer**
    Water Sign
    Cardinal Sign
    Symbol: The Crab

Cancer is primarily concerned with feelings and emotions. Cancer is the mother of the signs and, as such, is
the nurturing, maternal sign. Cancers love to take care
of people. This can be a problem because people will
sometimes take advantage of their giving nature. Cancers find it difficult to say no, but they need to learn this
lesson in order to save themselves from taking on other
people's problems.

Cancer is ruled by the Moon, and this makes Cancers
extremely sensitive emotionally. Their feelings are easily hurt, but they will hide hurt feelings behind a happy
exterior.

The symbol for Cancer is the crab, and this reflects
Cancer's traits in several ways. The crab moves side-
ways, and this shows Cancers' difficulty in taking a stand
on issues. Cancers will not strike out unless their homes
or families are attacked. The Sun was in Cancer when
the United States was formed, and our country did not
join World War II until U.S. soil was attacked directly
at Pearl Harbor. Like the crab, Cancers prefer to remain safe and secure in their shells.

Cancers' desire for security makes them homebod-
ies—more happy at home than out traveling.

One of the best examples of Cancer's nurturing nature is the character of Melanie in the movie *Gone with
the Wind*. The producers chose a Cancer actress, Olivia

de Havilland, to play the kind-to-a-fault Melanie. Equally wise was the choice of a Scorpio actress, Vivian Leigh, to play the sexy, manipulative Scarlett O'Hara.

The following Cayce reading seems to fit the traditional view that Cancer's influence is a maternal one, involving taking care of others.

We have afflictions in Cancer with the relationships in the Jupiterian forces. These make for those conditions where the strength of the body in its relationships to others has been and is spoken of rather in terms of that which is hushed in the manner of its greater expression.

In its associations with individuals, then, the entity becomes as a *helpfulness;* being a confidante of many; one to whom many come for their *own* instruction.   325-63

♌ Leo
Fire Sign
Fixed Sign
Symbol: The Lion

The sign of Leo involves generosity of spirit and the desire to be the center of attention. Leos love the spotlight and make natural performers in every arena. Leo is a kingly sign, which makes Leos powerful, majestic, and regal.

Leo is ruled by the Sun, the celestial body that provides the light and heat. Likewise, Leos can warm you with their fire or burn you to a crisp if annoyed. Beware of crossing swords with an angry Leo!

The symbol for Leo is the lion, and this royal animal is the physical embodiment of Leo's spirit. More than once Leos have come up to me and asked me to guess their sign. Upon saying, "Leo," they are always surprised. Their magnificent manes of hair always give them away—both male and female.

Leos love to be on stage even at an early age. Most people are terrified of public speaking, but the Leo daughter of a friend of mine insisted on performing at a local lecture series at the age of six. She could not stand not being in front of the audience.

Leo performers will be fiery, but in a stronger way than other fire signs. This is because Leo is also a fixed sign, but with the accompanying determination and consistency. They make loyal and giving friends as well.

In the human body, Leo rules the heart, and Edgar Cayce mentions this in the following readings:

> **We find that the present entity took its flight from that position of Mercury and with Venus, and in the sign of Leo, that has much to do with the worries mentally of the body in the earth's plane. That is, the mental worries of the present entity has to do more with conditions that are of the mental, or head forces, as in Leo, and of the heart than other conditions.   4313-4**

> **Thus these become part of the soul experience. As will be found, Leo—or the consciousness of that mind will be a part of the entity's awareness. Thus at times the entity will appear headstrong, willful; yet, as has been indicated, there are other influences of the benevolent nature (from Jupiter) making for the broadness, the bigness of the entity's abilities. In Venus combined with same, we find a great deal of color, a great deal of emotion, will be a part of the entity's experience.   2905-3**

♍ Virgo
Earth Sign
Mutable Sign
Symbol: The Virgin

The sign of Virgo is dedicated to the mental aspect of life rather than the emotional. Virgos are the perfectionists who cannot bear the slightest thing out of place.

Virgo is ruled by Mercury, the planet of the mind, so thoughts are more important to Virgos than emotions. This makes them great workers, but somewhat difficult to live with. You want a worker who spots every imperfection, but this trait is more difficult to deal with when the imperfection is in you. For example, I had a Virgo friend in high school who was a genius. He was valedictorian of our senior class and a brilliant student. When we would go somewhere together, he would ask me what time it was, and I would say, "It's 7:30." Then he would say, "Don't you mean 7:31?" This habit of his really irritated me, until I realized that he wasn't being picky or rude. That was just the way his mind worked. He could not accept anything, even the time of day, unless it was precise.

Because of their attention to detail, Virgos make excellent editors, technicians, scientists, etc. I have a friend who ran a small publishing company, and he had seven editors on his staff. Six out of the seven were Virgos. He said they were great at finding the smallest mistakes in manuscripts.

This analytical quality can sometimes lead to Virgos being unemotional and detached. This can be a particular problem in relationships. They need to realize that not every problem can be solved immediately and they need to allow patience and forgiveness to come into their personal relationships.

The great benefit that Virgos bring to a friendship is that they tend to be very steady emotionally. They don't have many highs and lows, and this can be stabilizing in a long-term relationship.

♎ Libra
Air Sign
Cardinal Sign
Symbol: The Scales

Libra is a sign that expresses itself through relationships. Libras are born diplomats, smoothing out the rough edges of human relations. Marriage, friendships, and family are of primary importance to Libras.

This sign is ruled by the planet Venus, so love is involved in all Libra relationships. Libras' desire for companionship is probably greater than any other sign in the zodiac. As a Libra friend of mine puts it, "Libras never meet a relationship that they don't like." Venus's rulership of Libra creates the need for beauty and harmony in those relationships.

Libra's symbol is the scales, and Libras are always weighing one side against the other. This can make them appear wishywashy. They need to learn to make a commitment and stick to it.

As an air sign, Libras need intellectual stimulation in their relationships. This intellectuality, combined with the Venus influence, can make Libras interesting and optimistic people.

One of my favorite examples of how Libra works involves the famous Libra general, Dwight D. Eisenhower. Eisenhower was supreme commander of the Allied forces in Europe in World War II and had to balance the needs of troops from many different countries. Two of his Allied subordinates were Field Marshall Bernard

L. Montgomery of Great Britain and General George
S. Patton from the United States. Both leaders were
Scorpios, both were prima donnas, and they disliked
each other. Eisenhower was able to balance these two
Scorpios and use them to gain a great victory. The ability to use diplomacy for the good of all is the great tal-
ent of Libras.

Edgar Cayce had this to say about the influence of
the sign of Libra:

> The symbols about same—Leo, Libra—repre-
> sent the mental expansion in Leo—in Libra, the
> being too liberal, as would be literally expressed,
> with self.   303-31

♏ **Scorpio**
   Water Sign
   Fixed Sign
   Symbol: The Scorpion

Scorpio is the sign whose key word is intensity. In
terms of emotion, no sign is as deep and powerful as
Scorpio. Whatever they commit themselves to, it is a
total commitment, so it is very important that Scorpios
choose the right path from the beginning.

Mars and Pluto are the rulers of Scorpio, so war,
death, and regeneration are no strangers to Scorpios.
They make excellent military leaders, doctors, and scientists because of their ability to look into the deeper
mysteries of life. These are the "old souls" of the zodiac.

Scorpio is a fixed sign and, because Pluto is one of its
rulers, no sign is as stubborn as Scorpio. The United
States Marine Corps, well known for toughness and
determination, falls under the sign of Scorpio. During
World War II the Germans called the marines the "devil

dogs" because of their tough fighting ability.

Scorpio is a water sign, and this shows Scorpio's deep emotional nature. But Scorpios will hide their emotions because of their great desire for secrecy. They often have a hidden agenda that no one ever sees.

One of the best examples of the Scorpio personality was General Patton. He was blunt, outspoken, and powerful, yet he was also so deeply spiritual that he wrote poetry, read the Bible every day, and believed in reincarnation.

Scorpios know no fear, so no sign is as vulnerable to potential choices between good or evil.

♐ **Sagittarius**
Fire Sign
Mutable Sign
Symbol: The Arrow

Sagittarius is the philosopher of the zodiac. It is more spiritually oriented than the other signs, interested in religious ideals, philosophy, and all codifications of thought in society. In spite of their deep thinking, Sagittarians still desire to be free spirits, not tied down by convention.

Sagittarius is a fire sign, so its mode of expression is energetic and dynamic. Like all fire signs, Sagittarians take the stage well, often projecting themselves into the performing arts. They need to be careful of hyperactivity for the fire that burns can burn itself out.

The symbol for Sagittarius is the arrow that flies straight and true, and this represents Sagittarian honesty and truthfulness. Sagittarians are straight talkers, but not in a blunt way like Scorpios. They say what they mean and mean what they say.

Sagittarius is the sign of travel to foreign lands, and

this is shown in the Sagittarius character. They love travel and the opportunity it gives them to experience different cultures of the world. Travel allows them to expand their awareness.

Jupiter's rulership of Sagittarius is shown in Sagittarius's desire to understand religion and the universal consciousness. All manners of religious thought appeal to Sagittarians, but less developed types can become dogmatic and narrow minded. Developing a broadminded philosophy of life is important for Sagittarius.

Edgar Cayce mentioned the spiritual aspect of Sagittarius's influence in the following reading for someone born on the cusp between the signs of Sagittarius and Capricorn.

> **In the aspects as we find them from the astrological sojourns, the entity comes close to the cusps.**
>
> **Hence they are in that position (through the signs!) that the influences are for the entity to be both a materialist *and* one given to spiritual things.**   **1869-1**

♑ **Capricorn**
   Earth Sign
   Cardinal Sign
   Symbol: The Goat

Capricorn is the business executive's sign. Capricorns are more interested in running the show than merely accumulating wealth. Capricorns are organized and conservative; you will never find a lazy person under this sign. They need to be careful, however, not to be overly materialistic. Ignoring the spiritual side of life can lead them into trouble.

Capricorn is an earth sign, and this leads to a practical, work-oriented approach to life. This also leads to appearing old even when they are young. I have a Capricorn friend who, even at an early age, always carried a briefcase. It was as if he had been preparing for his life in business even from grammar school.

Capricorns are methodical and precise in their work, and this can sometimes lead to perfectionist tendencies. The drive and ambition they feel needs to be tempered with an openness and flexibility. Working too hard can be as bad as hardly working.

Because Saturn rules the sign, Capricorns can sometimes feel they have the weight of the world on their shoulders. But it is this same Saturn that makes Capricorns such great organizers. They know how to find a place and a function for everything.

The symbol for Capricorn is the mountain goat, and this symbolizes Capricorn's drive to reach the top. It also shows the method Capricorns use to reach their goals—slow, steady progress upward, one step at a time.

Though they may appear outwardly cold, they can be great friends because they do not let their conservative nature stand in the way of friendship.

≈ Aquarius
Air Sign
Fixed Sign
Symbol: The Water Bearer

Aquarius is the sign that relates to groups and friendship. Aquarians are friendly to everyone in an impersonal way, treating everyone as equals. This is the great strength of Aquarius: to relate to everyone in a positive way, but not so closely as to be intrusive.

Aquarius is a fixed sign, so, once Aquarians get ideas in their heads, it is difficult to change their minds. This determination helps act as a rudder to guide Aquarians through the currents of life.

The traditional air sign emphasis on intellectuality is seen in Aquarius. They relate to people more on a mental level than on an emotional one. This can sometimes come off as an aloofness, but this is a sign that loves people. The Aquarian intellectual tendency will not get in the way of companionship.

It is also the sign of universal brotherhood, of love and respect for all. When I think of Aquarians, I think of a group of people holding hands and dancing around the campfire. This symbolizes the joy of a group helping and reaching out to each other.

The symbol of Aquarius is a man carrying a pitcher of water and pouring out that water as the source of life.

The following Cayce reading emphasizes the air-sign intellectuality of Aquarius:

> **Aquarius—making for the application of the mental self. Thus in Mercury we find the high mental abilities of the entity. And with those tendencies to analyze any given project, any given undertaking that may deal with the material world. Though the more oft the entity undertakes projects or undertakings when *others* should be considered *with* the entity, and a *cooperative* spirit manifested by the entity in doing so.   1265-1**

Another interesting Cayce reading tells us that Mary, the mother of Jesus, was an Aquarian.

> **As to the influences that arise from the astrological sojourns, these are rather in keeping with the time—the Aquarius forces, and as there are the beginnings of the Aquarian age.**

Then *do not* consider self as being unusual because unusual experiences arise in thy associations, in thy meditations, in thy activities with thy fellow men. Do not do *other*, though, than contemplate these. Remember thou art in the same signs, omens, as the Mother of Him; that gave to the earth the physical man, Jesus—Aquarius in its *perception*, perfection.   1222-1

)(**Pisces**
   Water Sign
   Mutable Sign
   Symbol: The Fish

Pisces is the sign of emotional sensitivity. Pisceans are the psychic sponges who absorb the thoughts and feelings of those around them. This works in a positive way in that it allows Pisceans to have an almost telepathic awareness of the thoughts of others. It works in a negative way when Pisces people absorb negative emotions created by themselves or those around them.

The sign of Pisces is ruled by Neptune, the planet of intuition and dreams, so it does not lend itself to making Pisces people practical or ambitious. Neptune's rulership of Pisces can help Pisceans drift with the flow so they are often in the right place at the right time, saying the right thing to the right person.

Pisces is the martyr's sign, and this can work in two ways. Either Pisceans can become consumed with self-pity and develop a martyr's complex, or they can happily sacrifice themselves for others. Pisceans can give themselves to others more than any other sign of the zodiac.

A water sign, Pisces is symbolized by the fish. This makes water and bodies of water very important to

Pisceans. Edgar Cayce was a Pisces, and he was told
that if he moved near the ocean it would help his psychic abilities. This led to his move to Virginia Beach,
Virginia.

Many of the traditional astrological traits of Pisces
appear in the following Cayce readings:

> As to such activities, then, we find the entity in
> the present is under the water sign, or Pisces.
> Hence to live near bodies of water, to be associ-
> ated in its activities with things having to do or
> to deal with the shipping business, or fishing
> business, or boat building, or the inter-com-
> merce of a larger scale, any of these in which the
> entity may interest itself will be found not only
> to be of aid and of interest, but to be remunera-
> tive to the entity in its experience in the sojourn.
> 798-4

> But the activities of the entity in the earth then
> become more impelling, for the entity in its very
> nature—as indicated by the Piscean influence—
> is sensitive to influences of the spiritual or astral
> as well as of the material natures.   1158-2

> As in Pisces makes for an interest in the oc-
> cult, in the mystic; and innate influences in same.
> 1226-1

> Coming under the Piscean sign makes for the
> water and activities over same, and near to same,
> as ever an influence in the experience.

> Hence we find Neptune as the greater influence.

> Hence the intuitive forces, the mystic influ-
> ences in the experiences of the entity; whether
> allowed to manifest by the activity of the mental
> abilities of the entity or not.

> Thus things that are of the mystic or mysteri-
> ous nature ever become a part of the entity's ex-

pression and manifestation in one form or another.   1506-1

As to the records of the astrological influences,
these are of the Piscean that make for the mystic, for the leaderships, for love and beauty, for
the abilities to direct; especially when self has
been conquered.   1346-1

Are the Signs Thirty Degrees Off?

The astrological sign positions used by most astrologers are based on the time of the year rather than the
position of the Sun with respect to the background stars
or constellations. What this means is that March 21 is
always 0° Aries regardless of whether the Sun is in the
constellation of Aries at the time. This approach is
known as the tropical zodiac system.

Another system, based on the actual position of the
Sun in the constellations, is known as the sidereal system. The Sun positions in the sidereal zodiac differ by
30° from the tropical system that most astrologers use.

This means that if your Sun is at 15° Libra in the
tropical system, the actual position of the Sun in the
constellations is 15° Virgo, exactly one sign back from
15° Libra. There is considerable debate about which
system should be used, but since the overwhelming
majority of astrologers use the tropical system, that is
the one we will use in this book to prevent confusion.

The Edgar Cayce readings indicate, however, that
the sidereal system is the one astrologers should be using:

For the Egyptian and the Persian records are
quite varied. If the entity would study astrology,
do not put the signs in the Egyptian calendar but
in the Persian, for the Persian interpretations are

more proficient than the Egyptian. This is not belittling the efforts of the entity nor of the Egyptians in those periods, but the variations in time have been corrected by the Persians and not by the Egyptians. The Egyptian calculations are thirty degrees off.   2011-3

For most astrologers are nearly thirty degrees off in their reckoning in the present.   3376-2

If one argues in favor of the tropical zodiac system based on the influence of the four seasons rather than the constellations (i.e., that Aries should begin at the first of spring because it is the first sign), this argument presents its own problem. March 21 is the beginning of spring in the Northern Hemisphere, but it is the beginning of fall in the Southern Hemisphere. So the seasons are reversed.

I believe that the signs are not nearly as important as the planetary sojourns, and I think this is reflected in how often the signs and the planets are mentioned by Cayce.

Below is a list of the number of times the signs and planets are mentioned in Cayce' s over 14,000 readings:

Pisces 129	Venus 2,210
Aries 96	Jupiter 2,205
Leo 74	Mercury 1,864
Gemini 57	Uranus 1,353
Aquarius 40	Sun 1,285
Scorpio 38	Mars 1,022
Libra 36	Saturn 975
Sagittarius 30	Neptune 591
Capricorn 18	Moon 460
Taurus 17	Pluto 83
Virgo 9	
Cancer 4	

The fact that the planets were mentioned so many more times than the Sun signs indicates that planetary sojourns are a much greater influence than signs, presumably because, between lifetimes, we experience the energies and dimensions of the planets, not the signs.

4

THE PLANETS

The Sun, the Moon, and the planets are the building blocks of astrology. The signs are important, but the planetary bodies have the greatest influence because that is where we experience our sojourns between lives. The aspects, angular relationships among the Sun, Moon, and planets, comprise the great power of astrology.

In this chapter we will examine the influences and characteristics of the individual planets and how they intertwine with our destiny.

Edgar Cayce gave the following reading that identifies the influences of the individual planets:

> **As in Mercury pertaining of Mind.**
> **In Mars of Madness.**
> **In Earth as of Flesh.**
> **In Venus as Love.**
> **In Jupiter as Strength.**
> **In Saturn as the beginning of earthly woes, that to which all insufficient matter is cast for the beginning.**

In that of Uranus as of the Psychic.
In that of Neptune as of Mystic.
In Septimus as of Consciousness.
In Arcturus as of the developing.   **900-10**

With Cayce's ideas in mind, let's look more deeply into the meanings of the individual planets.

The Planets and Their Meanings

⊙   **The Sun**
      The Ego

The Sun in a person's astrological chart represents his or her ego, self, and sense of self-awareness. The Sun is the source of all life on earth, absorbing matter and putting out energy, light, and heat. Very few people have planetary sojourns in the Sun, but it is possible.

The planetary aspects to a person's Sun position are critical to his or her character and destiny. This is particularly true if the Sun is conjunct (at the same position) with one of the planets. In that case, the Sun colors the person's personality with the influence of the particular planet. For example, if a person has Sun conjunct Venus, it might make him or her more feminine. If they have Sun conjunct Mars, it might make them more masculine. If they have Sun conjunct Neptune, it might make them attuned to the music of the spheres. Any Sun aspect, good or bad, can be the most important aspect in a person's chart.

In addition to representing the ego in the chart, the Sun represents a person's health and vitality, willpower and strength. Negative aspects to the Sun can indicate egotism, self-aggrandizement, or a proclivity to force the will on others. Positive aspects to the Sun can be indicative of an inner strength at the core of self. This strength characteristic of the Sun's influence is shown in the following Cayce readings:

> **Being under those influences of Moon and Sun also, we find in the Sun the strength and in the Moon the weakness.**   **2990-2**
>
> **The sun indicates strength and life, while the moon indicates change . . .**   **5746-1**

☽ The Moon
The Emotions

The Moon in a person's astrological chart has to do with his or her emotional nature. The gravitational pull of the Moon effects the oceans' tides and the tides of our emotional life as well. The fact that the word *lunacy* comes from the word "luna" or "moon" is no coincidence.

The Moon also reflects the mother in a chart, as well as relationships with women in general.

Some astrologers feel that the Moon is the only planet that is active in a person's childhood and that aspects to the Moon are the only ones active during that time period. In any case, the Moon definitely reflects the emotions, the mother, childhood, and the home life.

The key to the Moon's influence in the birth chart is in the aspects the Moon makes with the other planets. For example, a bad aspect from Neptune would create a tendency for emotional confusion, while a good aspect from Mars would create a tendency for positive emotional vitality.

Edgar Cayce's view of the Moon's influence is very similar to traditional astrological interpretations:

> **In Mercury, Venus, Jupiter and Uranus we find the greater activities. The Moon is only a portion of the experience, but it gives the greater emotion.**   **3089-1**

> For, as is seen, with the often change in the
> Moon's influence in the life is as to those condi-
> tions as have to do with those of the home, of the
> marital relations . . .   4286-3

> The Moon was a sojourn of the entity. Hence
> oft in the developing years, though beautiful in
> body and in manner of expression, in its associa-
> tion, the entity was always called fickle—or
> changeable.   1620-2

The Moon was such a great influence in one person's
life that Cayce told him not to sleep with the Moon's
light shining on his face.

> From the astrological aspects we find there
> was a sojourn upon the moon.

> Hence the moon is an active influence of the
> entity, and do not ever sleep with the moon shin-
> ing upon the face.   1401-1

Cayce emphasized that the Moon's influence had to
do with love affairs and sexual attraction.

> Through the moon's elements [we find these]
> bring the forces in love affairs to deter these con-
> ditions, one that is given to thinking lightly of
> the heart's forces—and should only be in domes-
> tic relations late in life, see?   900-6

> In Moon's influence in this entity has particu-
> larly to do with the earthly satisfaction of desire
> toward opposite sex, in the present plane's
> sphere.   900-14

> From the Moon we find the tendencies to-
> wards the love of the social life, which might eas-
> ily become a failing—because of its greater
> abilities as an individual. For, as indicated, the
> entity's personality will stand out in groups and
> among its associates in such a manner that all will

seek companionship with the entity.   2459-1

In traditional astrology the Moon in a "square" relationship (90 degrees) to Saturn is considered an aspect for depression and doubt, and this is shown in the following reading:

> **This brings the forces that gives the greater elements in the life, yet with the undue influence by the Moon's forces, when square to Saturn and Mars, brings doubts within the body's mental forces. In will's realm then must the entity bring the better forces when such conditions arise.**
>
> **137-4**

☿ **Mercury**
  The Mind

Mercury is the planet associated with the mind and mental reasoning. It also rules communication, contracts, and speech. A well-aspected Mercury indicates that a person can write and speak well.

The aspects to Mercury from other planets can be an indicator that a person takes a mental approach to communication. A Mercury-Mars aspect would indicate a person who is very direct and straightforward in speech. A Mercury-Venus aspect would indicate a person who speaks softly, with abilities for poetry, music, and the arts.

One of the things I often hear from people is that they are worried about the influence of Mercury when it is in retrograde motion (the apparent backward motion created by the relative orbits of the planets). There is nothing negative about a retrograde Mercury, because the aspects to Mercury are the most important elements. Whether it is retrograde or not, Mercury is neutral. The aspects from other planets color it good or bad. A badly aspected Mercury can indicate problems in thinking or communicating.

Edgar Cayce associates sojourns in Mercury with high mental abilities:

> In Mercury we find the entity high-minded, and at times all-knowing to its own undoing. At other periods we find the ability to think through, and to be a good conversationalist.   3478-2

> In Mercury we find the natural tend at times for the interest in things of the deeper nature; as books, as law of cause and effect in relationships with individuals or with groups.   2322-2

> In Mercury, then, we find the high mental abilities of the entity; the ability to speak well; the ability to meet others.   2381-1

> In Mercury—the high mental abilities; the practicality also of spiritual as well as mystical, as well as material things in the innate forces of the body; or the question ever, "For what purpose is this?"   1981-1

According to Cayce, between-life sojourns in Mercury give the soul the ability to process and communicate information:

> From the Mercurian influences we find the high mental abilities; tendencies in which the teaching or the abilities to impart to others become as a natural flow.   1626-1

> In Mercury we find one of high mental abilities, as indicated by the manner in which the entity—or present body—progressed, and progresses, in the ability to gather in *information* of any character or nature, as indicated in the work in the schools, as indicated in the work in associations with groups or individuals.   272-4

The influences in Mercury show a great mental ability, and a memory that if it is kept in a developing way and manner becomes rather unusual—as to data, as to facts or figures, as to statistical developments in any field in which it may be applied.   1252-1

Cayce also tells us that Mercury gives an analytical mind and executive abilities:

Mercury gives rather the analytical turn of mind . . .   358-3

From the Mercurian, naturally one of high mental executive ability.   437-2

From Mercury there are the high mental abilities, with *business* acumen; making for not only interest in individuals, people or conditions, but things also that have to do with the exercising of the rights of individuals.   319-2

Under Mercury, rather the high mental abilities; an aptness with lines, drawings, figures, and those things that materially have to do with such are of special interest.   322-2

Cayce reveals that at times a Mercury sojourn gives the ability to understand and deal with people:

The experience from Mercury makes for high mental abilities, the visioning, and the abilities to picturize or visualize those things in the experience of others that may make for the emotions arising in the activities of individuals.   954-1

In those applications in the Mercurian influence we find the high mental abilities, the desire at times to reason things out alone, the ability to be a good listener, and the ability to ponder things in its own mind.   1334-1

In Mercury we find judgment and consideration, and this with tolerance gives that ability for the entity to be companionable with whatever influence or environ in which it may find itself.

The entity is one well-liked, then, in any environ.   808-18

Cayce tells us that a negatively aspected Mercury produces a mind too quick to judge:

From Mercury we find one of high mental abilities; apt, quick in drawing conclusions—too quick at times.   997-1

From Mercury we find the high mental abilities, and yet these may at times cause rather harsh judgments.   958-3

♀ Venus
Love

The planet Venus is the planet of love and beauty. In a person's astrological chart, Venus symbolizes his or her love nature, and aspects to Venus can give clues as to how love will manifest in life.

In addition, Venus rules the love of music, nature, and the arts. People with a well-aspected Venus often have ability as musicians, artists, or stage performers. Venus influences give a gentleness of expression and an appreciation for the finer things in life.

Venus is the most feminine of all the planets, and people with a prominent Venus in their charts will appear more feminine, whether they are male or female.

Venus's greatest influence is in the area of love, romance, and sex. Any Venus-Mars aspect in particular can give someone a powerful sex appeal. A badly aspected Venus can indicate problems in finding love and lasting affection.

Edgar Cayce agrees with the traditional astrological view associating Venus with love and beauty:

In Venus, then—love, beauty; symmetrical forces in the body, the body mind, in the development of those conditions and things about the body; order, and versatility in the order of conditions.   255-5

In Venus we find that love influence, making for the conditions that bring for cheerfulness in the lives whom the entity may contact.   6-2

We find in Venus the material manifestations of those attributes of such an environment; love, mercy, patience, kindness, longsuffering.
                                                    1150-1

In Venus we find those influences of love in its more perfect form, that attracts and gives and makes for those very influences and forces that are of the spirit.   774-5

From the experiences in Venus, we find that love, kindness, gentleness, may bring out that which is best in the entity's self, innately—and in the abilities to *do* things.   768-4

Those activities in Venus make for the affability of the entity, and the abilities for the entity to make friendships, and to make lasting friendships.   416-1

Also from Venus' influence we find the entity is one that, in the acts of everyday affairs, is considerate of others; one with a high sense of honor, of justice, of those feelings that may be experienced by others with whom the entity may have personal or group experience.   342-2

Venus makes for a gentleness of manner, of mien, that is extraordinary in one with such vi-

tality, such purposes, such aims, such a breadth
of activity.   870-1

A planetary sojourn in Venus indicates abilities in
music and the arts according to Cayce:

> From Venus also will be seen abilities not only
> in the field of music but in the field of imagina-
> tive influences as well, and visions may often be
> to the entity—in its early experiences in this so-
> journ—as realities to the developing mental in-
> fluences of the entity.   314-1

> In the latent urges from the Venus influence
> we find an appreciation of the beautiful, in
> things, conditions and experiences, as well as in
> things that to the mental body represent that
> termed the arts in man's experience.   459-12

> In Venus we find that influence as makes for
> an even disposition, an artistic temperament, a
> love for the beautiful in ways and manners, that
> will these find expression in those fields that
> make for the expansion in the designing field . . .
>   451-2

Cayce tells us that Venus sojourns also give a love of
the beauty of nature:

> In Venus we find the lovely becoming the ex-
> pressions in activities in which there is the beauty
> seen in love, in companionship, in association, in
> music, in art, in *all* the things that bespeak of the
> *loveliness* even of nature and the material things,
> rather than the expression of same in the earthy
> form or manner.   949-13

> Also from Venus we find the love of the beau-
> tiful, even of the body-beautiful, of art, of nature,
> of all forms of activity as would pertain to the
> natural sources of beauty.   1074-2

In Venus we have that urge for everything beautiful—music, color, nature. The entity is especially one who appreciates nature's beauty—the snow, the rain, the sleet, the sunshine, the flowers, the green in the springtime, the color in the fall. All of these mean much to the entity, for it is sensitive to God's own expression in nature.
                                                        3356-1

Love and peace, as in Venus. Broadness of vision, and that which deals with things that grow. *Life*, as it manifests itself, becomes of the greater interest to the entity, and those things that will visualize—as it were—the beauties that are seen in nature as it opens to the blessings of the afternoon rain or the morning sun.   410-2

Further, Venus sojourns can also show a love of pets:

One who, from the Venus sojourn, is sympathetic; loving pets and those things that it may control or direct by its own very emotions; making for the abilities to create those environs which are befitting its activities and surroundings.   371-2

Cayce tells us that people who have had Venus sojourns know how to attract the opposite sex:

The Venus influences, as we find, make for the attractions that the entity has for those of the opposite sex, and those attractions that naturally are created by the activities and the gentlenesses and kindnesses (or especially the eyes) of the entity in relationships to those of the opposite sex. Beware that these do not bring in the experience the complexities or conditions that make for perplexing problems!   914-1

From Venus we find the very unusual experiences and influences of the entity in relationships to those of the opposite sex.   **1107-1**

Venus indicates that ability of the entity to attract the opposite sex when it desires and to shun same when desired. It also makes for the abilities as a good mother, a kind, patient, loving friend, a good companion, one appreciating beauty, kindness, gentleness; able to appreciate one who can administer same to others when desirous in such measures as to bind others to the entity. 3479-2

From Venus we find that making for the love of the beautiful; music, art in any of its phases; the desires oft for associations that in the experiences of many may appear as questionable.

622-4

The following Cayce reading is my favorite about Venus, because people often confuse passion with love:

In Venus we find love. Do not confuse affection with love. Do not confuse passion with love. Love is of God, it is creative, it is all giving.

3545-1

♂ Mars
Madness

The planet Mars in a person's astrological chart signifies energy and desire. Mars is the energizing principle in astrology, giving verve and vigor to any other planet it aspects. Mars is about action.

Mars is the most masculine planet, and people with a strong Mars will show masculine tendencies.

In mythology, Mars was the god of war, and this reflects the dangerous nature of Mars. Anger, violence, and war can result if Mars is badly aspected. In my experience as an astrologer, I have noticed many violent deaths coincide with a bad Mars transit.

Most of the time, however, a bad Mars aspect will result in a tendency to be overly aggressive, and this can sometimes lead to accident or injury.

A positively aspected Mars can indicate athletic ability. Research conducted by Michel Gauquelin in the mid-1950s found a direct correlation between a prominent Mars in a person's chart and success in athletics. Mars gives energy and strength.

The Edgar Cayce readings warn that sojourns in Mars reflect anger and wrath in certain people:

> **In Mars we find that of wrath or madness; a high temper oft is an urge to be supersensitive to those things that may make for *direct* control or those things pertaining to persons or to those as *related* to the persons.**   963-1

> **The influences from Mars make one of high temper, one that rages at some very trivial matter . . .**   280-1

> **In Mars we find at times anger, or not just having what's wanted at the moment upsets the entity. Curb this. Know that all comes to him who puts his trust in the all-powerful influence of love and harmony, the real poem of life, and then works like thunder for same!**   2337-1

> **The influence in Mars is rather that of wrath, war, might, main, domineering, dominating . . .**
> **   417-1**

The anger that can come from Mars sojourns can sometimes bring the danger of war and gun violence into the life if higher spiritual ideals are not also developed:

> **. . . for with the influence of Mars is that of wrath, fire, firearms, powders, explosions and riots. These the body must be wary of, should it**

desire to reach the mental, the development, the scope of experiences in present earth's plane . . .

Be not overcome then with the madness in Mars to bring detrimental to self, for this would be a weakness in flesh.   341-8

In the influences that bring for warnings, as seen in Mars and Vulcan—beware of fire, and especially of firearms, or explosives that take the form of body in same, as powders or of such elements. These may bring destructive influences.
                                                    1735-2

For the Martian influences, through the changes in the activities among men in war, in wrath, in blood even, have brought changes for the entity, in the experience rather as oft from without, as it might appear.   884-1

In Mars comes the danger of injury though accident:

One who has the influence in Mars, the destructive forces as come to bodily injuries to the body, as has been exhibited in the body, yet these coming rather from those of accidental nature than from those through which and by which the entity is at all times closely surrounded. 953-13

Sometimes a Mars sojourn can have a simultaneously positive and negative influence in a person's life:

For we will find from Mars not only those inclinations for anger, madness, ire to arise, but also the inclination for the inventiveness, the daringness . . .   2157-1

Mars indicates the quick temperament; quick to show resentments, quick to make for actions or decisions.   1292-1

For Mars represents and is the influence that makes for urges within the innate forces of an-

ger, madness, wrath, strength, endurance.
1182-1

Hence we find from the Martian influence one very determined; one very set, one very decided in likes and dislikes; one that makes friendships easily and just as easily breaks them unless they carry on; and is naturally, to be sure, a leader in its material and its mental associations. 1426-1

Also Mars makes for this great influence as has been indicated of orderliness, neatness, and those things that pertain to the bringing of experiences as to everything being under command or law and order. And too oft the temptation is for the entity to be the law and the order also.
1201-2

The following Cayce reading tells us that a positive Mars sojourn is unusual:

Also in Mars we find a benevolent influence for the entity, which is rather the unusual than the ordinary.   962-1

Q. *What is the significance of the planet Neptune now transmitting my natal Mars at 29 degrees of Virgo? To what is it trying to prompt me?*

A. Activity—as of Mars oft does! Hence, as indicated, these activities should begin when there has been the crossing—after the 21st or 22nd of March—if there will be the complete success for the body.   815-5

Mars—not as to anger, but as to activity. Not that the entity doesn't get mad—it does! most often at self, however.   289-9

We find from Mars that the entity has a very good temper; this isn't bad temper, but a *good* temper! One without a temper is in very bad shape, but one who can't control his temper is in still worse shape! The entity is one, then, who has learned to *hold* the temper . . .   1857-2

One in Mars we find excellent as to its abilities to "make good" in any field of activity chosen by the entity, and *naturally* energetic. However, the entity is one easily tempted to flare at those things at variance to the entity.   2706-1

In Mars we find the affability as well as the very active service of the entity in its associations or connections with others. These as we find are well. Most fortunate, then, are those who may count the entity as a friend.   3268-1

♃ Jupiter
Strength

In astrology, Jupiter is the planet of philosophy, religion, and spiritual strength. A well-aspected Jupiter shows a positive, optimistic attitude and an attitude of generosity and benevolence to society in general. A poorly aspected Jupiter can show dogmatic religious beliefs and an exaggerated sense of self.

Jupiter is about expansiveness. Its influence, both positive and negative, is always big. It is also associated with wealth and the accumulation of resources. Positive contributions to society bring good fortune and success in their wake.

Jupiter is the planet that rules travel, and people with a strong Jupiter influence love to travel. In business, this traveling can be involved with education, publishing, or writing.

Edgar Cayce links Jupiter sojourns with the universal consciousness, that awareness we all have of our connection with God:

With Jupiter we find a universal consciousness, an awareness of the universal forces.   289-9

In Jupiter we find the great ennobling influences, the broad-mindedness, the ability to consider others, the universal consciousnesses that are a part of the entity's unfoldment.   2890-2

In Jupiter we find one having a great influence upon the lives, the experiences, the activities of others—by choices made by the entity; and rarely fully conscious of how far-reaching such choices may be, in the experience of others.   2834-1

We find Jupiter also with its universal appeal for the weakling, for the unfortunate, for those not as well blessed with material things. These are natural tendencies in the emotional nature of the entity.   2829-1

As for the urges latent and manifested we find astrologically the influence from Jupiter. Thus the interest the entity has in giving of itself in service to others, disregarding its own personal pleasures. Remember, as indicated, no one gives a cup of cold water in His name without receiving a reward.   5018-1

According to Cayce, Jupiter is associated with a broadness of vision:

One, then, that, in the Jupiterian influence, has the *vision* of life in *many* of its phases.   1738-1

Coming under the influences of Jupiter, we find this makes for a broad vision.   790-1

We find that Jupiter as a ruling influence makes for the greatness of vision, the periods when there have been the visions of the entity making for an activity of its own that would astonish others, that would make for a place for

itself, making for a career. These have been a
portion of the entity's dreams.   798-4

In some cases, Jupiter's influence produces good luck
and protection from harm:

> Jupiter makes for the great expanse of experi-
> ence, the periods in the experience of the entity
> that would be called or termed by some "lucky
> periods."   954-1

> Jupiter is a ruling influence for protective in-
> fluences, when under extremes or those things
> as would arise from self-indulgence or from ac-
> cidents the entity would be as it were miracu-
> lously preserved from bodily injuries—or from
> mental aberrations.   1467-3

Cayce tells us that Jupiter sojourns indicate a tendency to deal with large groups of people or the
masses:

> Jupiter has made for not only the high enno-
> bling influence but the tendency for relation-
> ships that deal with large numbers of peoples.
>   189-3

> The influences in Jupiter we find as a great
> breadth, as a piling up—as it were—of associa-
> tions, meeting numbers and large numbers of
> individuals and groups.   694-2

> From the Jupiterian experience or influence
> we find the abilities as a leader or director, or
> one to whom many will come for counsel or ad-
> vice. And oft the entity, by its own quietness, in-
> vites confidences from others.
>
> Not that the entity is aloof, but the entity finds
> itself oft alone; yet influencing many groups or
> masses.   1895-1

We find in Jupiter the same type of influence as in its dealings or relationships to masses; as Jupiter represents that consciousness or activity of a universality of strength, of might, of power.
2420-1

In traditional astrology Jupiter rules the publishing industry, and Cayce, too, associates Jupiter with books and writing:

From Jupiter there is the universal consciousness, and the ability—when finding self—to *write!*   2530-1

Jupiter, then, makes for a broad experience; the activities in relation to things that will induce, promote, expression or thought in the minds of others. Its conjunction with the Mercurian influence would induce towards that of writing . . .
1096-1

Jupiter is an influence in the accumulation of wealth:

In those things in Jupiter we find material things coming into the hands of the entity . . .
1221-1

From the Jupiter influences there should be brought *moneys* and moneyed individuals into the environ and in the experience of the entity, through the mental application of self *mentally*.
620-1

In Jupiter we find the great expanse of experience that has come, and with its benevolent influences makes for those expressions of love the entity has or may show in its dealings with its fellow man; making for those innate expressions of that which is of the magnificent, that is of those that—if turned into those directions of the earth-earthy—become ones with power, ones with strength, ones with *affluence* in high and lowly places. 707-1

Jupiter influences make for the love of travel and people from other countries:

We find that the influences in Jupiter make for that urge wherein sometimes travel, change, or environs of many natures present themselves in the experience of the entity.   877-1

In those of the influences of Jupiter, we find these make for the expanse in the relationships, and the wide acquaintance, friendships, scenes, lands. Many will be those that will come *under* the influence *of* the entity.   1714-1

In Jupiter we find rather the tendencies and urges for the activities to be of the universal nature, or among the populace, or in associations with quite varied characters or groups, and in quite varied connections of other lands. 2476-1

In the Jupiterian we find makes for relationships with individuals of high position, of power or of fame or of fortune. These make for great expanse for travel, for those things that have to do with influences that touch the lives of many peoples.   1250-1

♄ Saturn
     Change

Saturn is the planet of discipline and responsibility in traditional astrology. It is the hard taskmaster that makes us face difficulties and overcome them through determination and hard work.

Bad Saturn aspects are the toughest ones in astrology. These aspects result in everything being swept away that we have depended on for security. Saturn is also referred to as the Lord of Karma.

Good Saturn aspects result in the fulfillment of long-term goals. A strong Saturn in a person's chart shows the ability to work hard for future gains. It is a quotient for emotional maturity.

Saturn in a birth chart gives clues as to how well a person will do in his or her career, and also what kind of career he or she will choose.

Saturn's reputation is that of the bad boy of the zodiac, but facing the severe limitations of Saturn can force a person to become organized and disciplined and develop the ability to bring order out of the chaos.

Astrologers often speak of a person's "Saturn return." It takes 29 years for the transiting Saturn to move around the Sun and return to the position it held on the day of a person's birth. This 29th year of a person's life can give clues as to how well aspected his or her natal Saturn is. A well-aspected Saturn in the birth chart will provide a very positive Saturn return. A negatively aspected Saturn in the birth chart can create difficulties in the 29th or the 58th year.

Edgar Cayce's view of Saturn differs slightly from traditional astrology. Cayce says that Saturn represents change:

We find in Saturn the changes, the experiences that have brought divisions, disturbances; breaking into the hopes, the aspirations, the desires.

2401-1

In Saturn we find the sudden changes that have appeared, and do appear, in the experience of the entity. For, as has been the experience, not only in the joys of living but in the companionships that have been thine through this experience, there have come suddenly—and apparently with-

out warning—changes and separations. 2281-1

From Saturn's influences we find the changes that have arisen, when there have been periods of great exaltation, periods of depression, periods when the physical as well as the mental and material were under a stress and strain of adverse forces—being the natural consequence of the influence of Saturn's activity in the experience of an individual in the material plane.   1010-12

A between-life Saturn sojourn can create problems for people in that they desire constant change and are not able to follow anything through to its completion:

From Saturn we find the tendency for the starting of new experiences, the starting of new associations in the activities; and unless these are tempered with the mental influences they are rarely carried to their full termination.   361-4

Just so do we find that Saturn's forces have brought, do bring, the sudden changes, the questionable influences, the things which the entity must constantly eradicate as it were from itself; whether as a thought, or a habit, or an associate, or an environment; and begin as it were all over again.   1597-1

The experiences in Saturn make for a tendency to be rather changeable, or always stating something new, or inclinations for "Today I would like to do this," and tomorrow, "Well, I would like something else." These are inclinations. Hence must be met in the mental and the spiritual forces of self.   781-5

In those astrological forces as indicated from Saturn and its influence in the entity's activities in the present, we find the tendency for change, the tendency for commencing over again, the

tendency to feel within self "Could I but blot out
this, could I but change that" these would make
for differences in the activities in the relationships, the activities in the purposes. But how hath
He given in His promises, in His judgments?
"Use that thou hast in hand." And as ye use this,
then may there be given thee the next step.

1220-1

In his readings, Cayce described Saturn as "that
planet to whom all insufficient matter is cast from
the earth plane" (5717-1). What did he mean by this?
He meant that those souls who have done evil on
the earth are sent to Saturn to be remade. No soul is
ever lost unless the soul wills it, but souls that are far
from God in the earth plane are sent to Saturn to
lose their individuality. The slate is wiped clean, and
they are made over. This is why souls with a Saturn
sojourn want change: They have just been changed
themselves!

To this body nothing is ever lost. Far from the
influence of Saturn, that planet to whom all insufficient matter is cast from the earth plane.

5717-1

Saturn is that realm to which all insufficient
matter is cast for remoulding. This rules the entity mostly. But know that no urge of any soul
exceeds the will of self, that which makes you as
an individual different from all other individuals.
For no one can touch the soul nor add to nor
take from it, other than by thy will allowing such
to be done. 3545-1

According to Cayce, Saturn influences bring disappointments, discouragements, and sorrow:

For, disappointments as indicated in Saturn

have been and *will* be a part of the experience.
3268-1

We find in Saturn the changes that come—
those periods in which the entity may become
easily discouraged, and weep. But remember, He
gave expression in such a manner; weeping with
those who wept, rejoicing with those who did
rejoice.   2571-1

We find in Saturn that discouragements easily
arise in the experience at times; the determination to be or do, and yet losing the purpose before the activities have reached that as desired.
Thus the entity becomes at times too easily discouraged.   2636-1

In the influences then of Saturn and Uranus,
there are troubles brought into the life, and tri-
als through those of the secular nature, and much
sorrow in the life.   265-1

In Saturn we find the sudden or violent
changes—those influences and environs that do
not grow, as it were, but are sudden by that of
change of circumstance, materially, or by activities apparently upon the part of others that become a part of self in the very associations. And
yet these are testing periods of thy endurance, of
thy patience, of thy love of truth, harmony and
the spirit that faileth not.   1981-1

Sometimes a Saturn sojourn will produce a love of
travel and changing scenes:

In Saturn we find the love for change, for
change of scene; the love of travel, the love of
being quite busy at all times or seasons, with only
the periods of relaxation as necessary for the
beneficial influences.   2029-1

> In Saturn we find the sudden changes in envi-
> rons, in surroundings—the desires to see far
> fields—or, as oft expressed, far away fields ap-
> pear the greener.   **1946-1**

A Saturn sojourn can be made a good thing by people
who are able, when given a lemon in life, make lemon-
ade:

> We find in Saturn the changes, and order. The
> entity is orderly in its person and its relation-
> ships.   **5154-1**

> In Saturn we find the sudden changes that have
> been in the experience of the entity, not only
> from the material but from the mental and spiri-
> tual aspects also. This, too, is unusual. For, the
> entity has used the varied influences as stepping-
> stones the more oft, and not as stumbling-
> stones—as most Saturn and Mars individuals do.
>   **1757-2**

Edgar Cayce often said that an obstacle in your path
can be either a stepping-stone or a stumbling block,
depending on how you approach it. The key to overcoming Saturn problems is developing the ability to
embrace change.

♅ Uranus
The Psychic

Uranus is the planet of originality, freedom, and eccentricity. People with a powerful Uranus in their chart
desire freedom at all costs. No rigid structure will hold
these people back from expressing themselves.

They express themselves in very unusual ways. They
are not tied by tradition, and at their best, their different ways of thinking can create new inventions and new

ways of doing things. They are often called geniuses.
The negative influence of Uranus can make people tend
to be "way out" or "kooky." If intelligence can be conceived as a circle, then genius is right next to idiot.

In terms of career, Uranus rules astrology, aviation,
electronics, television, and computers. Because they are
slow moving, Uranus and Neptune have been conjunct
all through the 1990s. As a result, we have seen an explosion of growth in the field of electronics.

This Uranus-Neptune conjunction has also created
great opportunities for an opening of global awareness
for the people on earth. In a positive way worldwide
telecommunications has made people more aware of
everything that is happening on earth.

Uranus rules the occult and astrology, and there has
been a growth of interest in these fields in recent years.

Edgar Cayce tells us that Uranus is the planet of extremes:

> Uranian influences are for the *extremes;* very
> high, very low in the phase of human endeavor
> or human experience.   949-13

> In those in Uranian makes for these *extremes*
> in likes and dislikes.   2111-1

> Under Uranus—one exceptional in abilities,
> whether that of the mental or of physical endur-
> ance, or application of either.   220-1

> In Uranus we will find the extremes indi-
> cated—even in the temperaments of a very de-
> mure, meek entity; and then one almost *wild* at
> times in its determination for its own way; and it
> knows *what* it wants and not any questions!!
>   1566-3

This tendency toward extremes in Uranians creates
up-and-down situations in life:

Here we find an entity (in urges) almost a full Uranian. Hence we will find many contradictory emotions, many contradictory activities oft manifested in the experiences—mentally and materially.

We will find periods in the purely physical during which *everything* will apparently work in a most harmonious way and manner, when *everything* seems—as it might be termed "to come the entity's way." Yet there will be experiences when there is quite the reverse, when nothing—physical, mental, social or in any manner—apparently has that reaction desired by the body.   1885-2

As indicated or accredited, the influence of Uranus or the Uranian indwelling in the experience of each soul makes for extremes in temperament, in enthusiasm, in zeal, or in hate, or in any of those things that are the result of—or manifestation of—the experiences of the spirit of truth, or the spirit of self-indulgence or self-aggrandizement.   524-2

This produces contradictory forces, that are indicated in Uranus—the extremes to which the entity goes at times, either in one or the other direction, and at times both directions at once.
                                                   289-9

The following readings show that sojourns in Uranus tend to make a person more sensitive to the feelings and vibrations of others:

For, the Uranian influence we find makes for the innate "sensitive" individual; capable of discerning in the vibrations or feelings or emotions that are experienced by the entity in associations of individuals, or in the associations of even groups . . .   540-1

> One that is a Uranian, that is influenced for the extremes, is necessarily supersensitive—in the fingers as well as in every form of mental development.   **1978-1**

A Uranian sojourn brings an interest in psychic ability and occult subjects:

> The Uranian influence we find makes for a high occult or psychic force; or *soul* force, rather than the ordinary term of psychic.   **938-1**

> In Uranus is seen those of the occult and mystic nature, tending to either raise one's vision to a high degree or groveling in the slough of despondency.   **115-1**

> The entity is an Uranian; one very psychic, and very much given to search out mysteries of all natures; one who may make a very wonderful success in this experience or a real mess of it all.   **2476-1**

> There are the tendencies from Uranus towards the occult and the mystic forces; as visions, hearing, seeing and knowing without having the physical contact with experiences in the *mental* body.   **361-4**

> In the Uranian we find the interest in the mysterious or the occult, or those influences that come from out of nowhere—as it appears to those who are material-minded.   **1349-1**

Traditional astrology tells us that Uranus rules astrology, and Cayce agrees with this:

> Also in Uranus we find the abilities in directions pertaining to the study of astrological influences or associations, but especially as related to the analyzing of emotions.   **1595-1**

Cayce said many times in his readings that individuals who have had past lives in Atlantis have Uranian sojourns between lives. Cayce also said that many former Atlanteans are incarnating at the present time and that this is a parallel time in history to the time of Atlantis. Therefore, we now have a time of extremes and high technology, especially in the field of electronics:

That they would have mechanical application of electrical forces, to be sure, is another of those indications of not only the Uranian but the Atlantean experiences of the entity.   1747-3

As we find indicated, there are those latent forces from the Uranian as well as the Atlantean sojourn that make the entity the more sensitive than the ordinary individual.   2537-1

♆ Neptune
The Mystic

Neptune is the planet of mysteries and mysticism. In positive aspect, it gives the dreams and visions that inspire us to do great things. In negative aspect, it gives the confusion and delusion that leads us down the wrong path.

People with bad Neptune aspects can be victims of alcohol or drug abuse. Positive Neptune aspects provide intuitive understanding of the spiritual mysteries of life. This understanding often comes in the form of powerful and prophetic dreams, since dreams fall within the realm of Neptune's influence.

In mythology, Neptune was the ruler of the sea, and the planet Neptune is the ruler of liquids and large bodies of water.

In the career world, a prominent Neptune can lead a person to a job in chemistry, the movies, or anything involving the ocean or large bodies of water.

Neptune, however, is not considered the planet of the practical. It is more for the dreamers, the mystics, and the intuitives.

Edgar Cayce tells us that Neptune sojourns lead people to seek out the mysteries of life:

> **In Neptune we find also that consciousness of one well adapted in the unusual or the mysteries or the mysticism. These again are of the soul and are of the spiritual nature.   5082-1**

> **In those influences seen in those of Neptune, brings for those of that as is of the *mystery* in the experiences of the entity; the associations in many peculiar circumstances and conditions . . .
>   243-10**

> **Coming under the influence of Neptune then, as we find, makes for the mystic forces in the experience of the entity; as liking and loving a mystery (which may be seen even in the development in the tender years); liking to make a mystery of that it finds it is, or those that it would meet, in soft whispers, in creeping about, in finding those varied things that would make for such tendencies—these are quite evident in the present development.   398-1**

Neptune sojourns bring an interest in the spiritual:

> **Neptune brings the greater spiritual life, greater desire for the spiritual emotions than the purely material.   1986-1**

> **Neptune brings also comforts; not in material things, rather in the spiritual—and the inclinations produced in the experience of the entity as the emotions or interests in those things of a psychic or spiritual nature.   1493-1**

Those influences in Neptune and the Moon make for the interests in those of spiritual influence, mysticism and rites.   355-1

The spiritual influences of Neptune often come through dreams and visions:

We find in Neptune the visions, dreams, hopes, aspirations; and things having to do with air, water, and the elements *beyond* the realm of the earth.   2403-1

In the application of the influences, we find in that of Neptune, and of the influences in the occult—these bring for *unusual* experiences in visions, in dreams, and in that of occult and mystic forces.   543-11

Traditional astrology tells us that Neptune rules large bodies of water, and Cayce agrees with this:

Neptune makes for love of water.   1179-2

These are from *innate* experiences that go deeper; but, as is seen, the body itself is *supersensitive*—or one that may be said to be in that environ or strong influence of Neptune. Hence the body, rather than being inland, should dwell or sojourn near or upon large bodies of water; this would change the influences or bring about and into the experience of the entity those things that would be of a higher spiritual and mental nature.   620-1

The inclination of the entity from the natures of Neptune is for psychic influences or forces to arise.

Hence we will find that certain characters of waters—as springs, lakes, rivers—become as music in the creative forces, through which the entity may employ words to show the attunement

to which the soul may arise in giving expression.
                                                    1463-2

Cayce also gave warnings to people who had sojourns
in Neptune to stay away from large bodies of water:

> From the Neptune influences—keep away
> from large bodies of water!   2005-1

> In Mercury we find the high mental abilities;
> as in the watery planet—or in the activities of
> Neptune—we find beauty of body and the ex-
> pressing of same if it is in activity, yet this is a
> warning also—as it brings this character of expe-
> rience:
> Do not be too *daring* in the water, else we may
> bring a cutting short of the opportunities and
> experiences in the present sojourn.   1339-2

> From Neptune also we find the aversion to
> water and waterways, water activities; and yet
> there has not been a greater entity to sail the seas
> than this entity—in the experiences through the
> sojourn just previous to the present.   2157-1

> As to the warnings; that come from the Nep-
> tune influence:
> Do not invest moneys in any field that has to
> do with boats or maritime affairs, or things upon
> the water. Be very careful of water, or in endan-
> gering self by many trips in small crafts over
> same. Or else we will find its demands upon the
> *physical* abilities, the physical effect of the body
> itself.   1528-1

Neptune rules liquids and chemistry, and Cayce
points this out in the following readings:

> Also from Venus and Neptune we find that
> things of the chemical natures would also have

their latent urge in the entity's experience.

2925-1

The interests from the Neptune sojourn make for the love of the mystery, and that which will pertain unto the mysteries in the earth—or those as the relationships towards which the body-mind throughout its intent and developments in the earth has been inclined; those things that have made for the change in the mysterious forces in individuals, groups and masses; hence those things that pertain to the chemical world or those that pertain to the chemical-electrical world that give life and take life in the *elemental* forces of the activities in a material world. 640-1

♇ Pluto
Consciousness

Pluto is the planet of willpower, death, and regeneration. If it is in negative aspect in a person's chart, it gives a tendency toward dictatorial attitudes. In positive aspect it gives a subtle understanding and a deep penetrating awareness.

Pluto is also the planet of mass destiny. For example, many of the men who were elected president of the United States in the last forty years had positive Pluto aspects when they were elected.

The classic example was Richard Nixon. When he was elected in 1968, he had a positive Sun-Pluto relationship. In 1974, when he was forced from office, transiting Pluto had moved into a negative Sun-Pluto relationship.

In the scientific world, Pluto rules atomic energy. The Hiroshima bomb was exploded on August 6, 1945, when the Sun was conjunct Pluto.

Edgar Cayce gave readings that mentioned Pluto before it was officially discovered in 1930. He called it Vulcan or Septimus. So, the readings have three names for Pluto—Pluto, Vulcan, and Septimus.

Cayce gave readings to very few people who had sojourns in Pluto. This may be because it is a developing influence, and, according to Cayce, not one already established:

> Q. *Just what are the effects of Pluto, in conjunction with one's ascendant?*
>
> A. This as we find is entirely amiss from what we might call a physical expression—but, as we find indicated, these are a development that is occurring in the universe, or environs about the earth—Pluto. Not as some have indicated, that it is gradually being dissipated. It is gradually *growing*, and thus is one of those influences that are to be as a demonstrative activity in the future affairs or developments of man towards the spiritual-minded influences, or those influences outside of himself.
>
> These in the present, as might be said, are merely the becoming *aware* of same. Rather within the next hundred to two hundred years there may be a great deal of influence upon the ascendancy of man; for it's closest of those to the activities of the earth, to be sure, and is a *developing* influence, and not one already established.
>
> **1100-27**

Cayce agrees with traditional astrology in connecting Pluto (Septimus) with the will.

> . . . [Septimus], these we see deal with those as governed by the force and will . . .   5717-2
>
> . . . also from those of Septimus, which bring

the relations to the body under some conditions
that have passed, and are to be presented in the
future and which may be met by the will of this
entity.   **4227-1**

In traditional astrology, Mars and Pluto (Vulcan) in
bad aspect can be very dangerous, and Cayce seems to
confirm this in the following reading:

**In the influences that bring for warnings, as
seen in Mars and Vulcan—beware of fire, and
especially of firearms, or explosives that take the
form of body in same, as powders or of such elements.   1735-2**

Arcturus
The Developing

The readings tell us that in addition to the planets,
we can also have between-life sojourns on the fixed
stars. The star Arcturus is the ultimate achievement in
planetary sojourns. Arcturus is a red giant 113 times
brighter than our Sun. It is about thirty-six light years
from earth in the constellation Boötes. Arcturus is not
mentioned in traditional astrology, but it is very important in Cayce's story of astrology.

Cayce tells us that once a soul has achieved perfection in the earth plane, it goes to the star of Arcturus
and from there on to other systems.

**For, as long as an entity is within the confines
of that termed the earth's and the sons of the
earth's solar system, the developments are within
the sojourns of the entity from sphere to sphere;
and when completed it begins—throughout the
music of the spheres with Arcturus, Polaris, and
through those sojourns in the outer sphere.**
                                                  441-1

In this we find the relations as given from
those spheres in the earth's sphere; that is, as in
Mercury, as in Venus, as in Mars, as in Jupiter, as
in Earth, as in Uranus, as in Neptune, and the
chancing, or changing, as it were, from one development to another, until the entity passes
from that solar system, or sphere, through Arcturus or Septimus, as we see.   900-25

As an entity passes on, as has been given, from
this present—or *this* solar system, *this* sun, *these*
forces, it passes through the various spheres—
leading first into that central force, through
which—known as Arcturus—nearer the Pleiades,
in this passage about the various spheres—on
and *on*—through the *eons* of time, as called—or
space—which is *one* in the various spheres of its
activity; even passing into the inner forces, *inner*
sense, may they again—after a period of nearly
ten *thousand* years—may an entity enter into the
earth to make manifest those forces gained in *its*
passage.   311-2

The Cayce readings tell us that Arcturus is a great
sun around which the activity in this environ rotates:

Also we find the Sun and Arcturus, the greater
Sun, giving of the strength in mental and spiritual elements toward developing of soul and of
the attributes toward the better forces in earth's
spheres.   137-4

For Arcturus is that junction between the
spheres of activity as related to cosmic force, and
is that about which this particular environ or
sphere of activity rotates, or is a relative source
of activity.   263-15

The way to achieve perfection and a sojourn to Arcturus is to conquer self:

In a word, *much* has been made of the *present* experience, and it will lie within the own desire of the entity as to whether the return in earth's experience becomes necessary or not; for in Arcturus' forces, these become all magnified in will's force, and the conquering of self is truly greater than were one to conquer *many* worlds, and *is* conquering those of *our,* or of our *sun's* own attributes.   115-1

Arcturus is the opposite of Saturn. Perfected souls go to Arcturus, while souls that need reforming go to Saturn:

Also the relationship of the sojourn in the various elements that have to do with the spheres as related to earth's sphere—the variations from one passing through Arcturus to other forces, or returning to Saturn!   256-1

Once a soul goes to Arcturus, it has a choice either to go on to other systems or to return to earth to help. Edgar Cayce had to make this choice after his past lifetime as a Persian leader named Uhjltd (pronounced *yoolt*).

Q. *The sixth problem concerns interplanetary and inter-system dwelling, between earthly lives. It was given through this source that the entity Edgar Cayce, after the experience as Uhjltd, went to the system of Arcturus, and then returned to earth. Does this indicate a usual or an unusual step in soul evolution?*

A. As indicated, or as has been indicated in other sources besides this as respecting this very problem—Arcturus is that which may be called the center of this universe, through which individuals pass and at which period there comes the choice of the individual as to whether it is to re-

turn to complete there—that is, in this planetary
system, our sun, the earth sun and its planetary
system—or to pass on to others. This was an unusual step, and yet a usual one.   5749-14

Not that the sun that is the center of this solar
system is all there is. For the entity has attained
to that realm even of Arcturus, or that center
from which there may be the entrance into other
realms of consciousness. And the entity has chosen in itself to return to the earth for a definite
mission.   2823-1

Arcturus comes in this entity's chart, or as a
central force from which the entity came again
into the earth-material sojourns. For, this is the
way, the door out of this system. Yet purpose-
fully did the entity return in this experience.
                                              2454-3

But beginning with Mercury, the entity has
run the gamut even unto Neptune and Arcturus,
and then returned to earth.   3637-1

Finally, Cayce gave the following poetic description
of the beauty of an Arcturian sojourn:

In those experiences of the entity in its dwell-
ings in the hills and the plains of Persia, also in
Egypt, the beauties and music of the spheres
sang and brought into the experience of the entity its studies of the light by day, the joy of the
voices of the night, and the star that led the entity—that source from which and to which it may
gain so much of its strength in the present; *Arcturus*, the wonderful, the beautiful! As the bright
and *glorious* light from same set afire, as it were,
its meditations in the plains, so may the illumi-
nations do the same in the lives of those the entity contacts through its gentleness and kindness

and service. For he that would gain the understanding *pours out,* even as upon the desert sand,
that refreshing liberation of the spirit of truth
that rises to the Throne of grace as sweet incense
before the Giver of life and light and understanding, and immortality in Him!   827-1

Physical Characteristics of the Planets

One of the most fascinating things about the Sun,
the Moon, and the planets is that their influences fit
very well their physical characteristics. For example, the
Sun's influence has to do with the ego and strength. Its
enormous size and energy make it like the central ego
of the solar system.

The Moon's influence in astrology is the emotions,
and it is easy to compare the Moon's gravitational pull
on the oceans with the ebb and flow of human emotion.

The same is true of the planets. Mercury is the planet
of the mind. Using your mind requires mental concentration—dense thought, if you will. In terms of physical
mass, Mercury is the densest planet, which means it has
the greatest concentration of matter.

Venus is a loving, receptive, and feminine planet.
Venus's atmosphere is predominantly carbon dioxide,
so 90 percent of the light that Venus receives is absorbed
before it reaches the surface. This makes it the most
receptive planet. Venus is also a hot planet, and this fits
in with the idea of the warmth of love.

Mars is the planet of anger, aggression, and wrath,
and is red in color. People, when they are angry, talk
about "seeing red." Red is a lower frequency vibration
color, one that is associated with the lower vibratory
centers of the human body, including the adrenals, the
glands of fear, and flight.

Jupiter is the planet of benevolence, bigness, and expansiveness. It is the largest planet in the solar system, hundreds of times larger than earth. It is also the only planet that puts out more energy than it takes in.

According to Edgar Cayce, Saturn is the planet of change. The winds on Saturn blow at 1,500 miles an hour, the strongest winds in the solar system. Cayce also describes what he called the "Saturn winds" on the earth. This was Cayce's way of telling us that Saturn's influence causes powerful wind storms on the earth.

Uranus is the planet of eccentricity and extremes. This fits Uranus's physical nature well. Uranus's axis of rotation is 90° off from the plane of the ecliptic. If the plane of the ecliptic were a tabletop, Uranus would look as if it fell over. It is the only planet in the solar system with such a strange axis of rotation.

Neptune is the planet of water and the oceans. Neptune is bluish in color, and this matches the color of the oceans.

Pluto is the planet of will, death, and regeneration. Very few people who had readings from Cayce had sojourns in Pluto. This is understandable since Pluto is very small (it is actually smaller than some of Jupiter's moons) and is billions of miles from the earth. It, therefore, does not have a strong physical presence in the solar system.

The Future of Astrology

With respect to planetary sojourns, Cayce suggested that a questionnaire be developed that could ascertain what a person's planetary sojourns were. I think that it is easy for us to imagine, when reading the characteristics of the individual planets, which traits fit us and which do not. Therefore, an alternative to determining planetary influences from an astrological chart could be to fill out a questionnaire that would match up personal characteristics with those of the various planets. Cayce discusses this idea in the following reading:

> **As indicated, there may be charts drawn of five individuals, and a questionnaire may be determined for factors in the individual experience— as to what their inclinations or activities are. Not by telling, but by questioning!**
>
> **Then *from* same, as indicated, there may be given a more correct or direct questionnaire that would be helpful for a large *number* of individuals—but *not* a perfect score.**
>
> **For in about twenty percent of the populace at the present time, it is dependent upon what the individuals have done with their urges *through* material sojourns.   5753-3**

In the above reading, Cayce tells us that in about 20 percent of the populace, the astrological charts do not reveal the correct influence because of what people have done with their lives here on earth. The other 80 percent, he says, would be greatly helped by using astrology for vocational guidance:

> **The astrological aspects may give a tendency, an inclination; and a systematic, scientific study of same would indicate the vocation. And about eighty percent of the individuals would be in the position of being influenced by such astrological aspects; or would be in the position for their abilities to be indicated from same.**
>
> **But the other twenty percent would not be in that position, due to the influences from activity or the use of their abilities in material experience. Hence in these it would be not only necessary that their material sojourns be given, but as**

to what had been accomplished through same, and that to be met in the present experience. For, as has been indicated, no influence—astrologically or from material sojourns—surpasses the will or the determination of the individual. Then, there are material factors that rule or govern or direct or influence such forces. These may be tempered by the astrological aspects, but these are not (the astrological aspects) the major influence or force—the will.

Thus, only about eighty percent of the individuals may have their abilities indicated from the astrological aspects in the direction of vocational guidance, as to be a determining factor for such.   5753-3

Eighty percent of people can be helped by studying their astrological chart, but the interpretation of the chart is aided by an astrologer's own psychic ability, according to Cayce:

Q. Can a teacher or course of study be suggested which will impart this knowledge to me?

A. The knowledge may be had from many books, rather than from teachers. Teachers give only their *own* interpretation, as each individual makes his own aligning or adjusting of ideas as he studies same. And the correctness or suitableness of the information received depends upon the sensitiveness of the individual studying same, and the application of his own psychic faculties in making the divination of those influences that may be presented by such astrological positions or activities.   816-6

In these readings, Cayce has outlined for us the future of astrology. Three factors will be used in interpretation: (1) the astrological aspects of the chart itself; (2)

a questionnaire to determine astrological sojourns; and (3) the psychic ability of the astrologer who interprets it.

The Questionnaire

With Edgar Cayce's suggestion that a questionnaire be developed to determine a person's past planetary sojourns, I have put together the following list of characteristics for use in determining them.

By looking at these groups of key words and phrases and marking them in the order you think they best apply to you, you can determine the most likely planets of your past planetary sojourns.

1. Philosophical. Broadminded. Universal in approach. You are lucky and a leader; you love travel and foreign cultures. You deal with the masses and people in power and have broad vision. You are ministerial and appreciate the universal consciousness. You are a merchant and/or have good fortune. You like wealth, writing, publishing, and have many friendships.

2. Supersensitive. You have extremes in temperament—good or bad. Things go perfectly at times, but other times they go horribly wrong. You are interested in electronics, television, computers, aviation, the occult, astrology, or Atlantis. You are psychic and independent.

3. Loving and kind. You love music, the arts, beauty, and nature. You are cheerful, friendly, and gentle. You admire the "body beautiful." You are fashionable, a good decorator, sociable, attractive to the opposite sex, a good dancer, entertaining, and tend to be feminine.

4. Energetic, angry, athletic. You are interested in exercise, the military, guns, and fire. You have a high temper and quick temperament, but are strong, inventive, dar-

ing, active, neat, orderly, and determined. You are a hard worker, perhaps a surgeon, a soldier, a mechanic, and tend to be masculine.

5. Desire for constant change. You are sometimes unable to complete things. You experience separation, sudden changes, depression, disappointments. You feel the desire to start over and have much sorrow, discouragement, and change in your life.

6. Willful, aware, forceful. You are interested in physics, atomic energy, penetrating insight, and higher consciousness.

7. Dreamer, mystic, intuitive. You are spiritual, love the water (oceans, lakes, rivers), sailing, boats, chemistry, mysteries, alcohol, drugs, illusion, delusion, religious rituals, and poetry.

8. High mental abilities. Intellectual, executive, editorial, bookkeeper, lecturer, scientist, writer, student, thinker, teacher, publisher, lawyer, communicator. You can sometimes be quick to judge and have a good memory.

Now take your list and compare it to the key below:
1. Jupiter
2. Uranus
3. Venus
4. Mars
5. Saturn
6. Pluto
7. Neptune
8. Mercury

The top four planets in your list are the ones you most likely experienced between lifetimes. The bottom four are the ones with which you have had the least experience. Try showing the list of characteristics to your friends and have them rate those that most apply to you. Then see how the two lists compare. This will help you learn about your own past-life planetary sojourns.

5

THE ASPECTS

One of the most powerful tools in astrology is the angular relationships the planets make to each other, known as "aspects." Their positions being determined from tables in a book called an ephemeris, the Sun, Moon, and planets are laid out on a circular chart with the earth as the center. The angular relationships between the bodies on this circle are then calculated. (See Chart No. 4.)

Certain degrees of angle have great significance in astrology, the most important of which are: conjunctions, sextiles, squares, trines, and oppositions. A margin of plus or minus 6° (called the "orb") is acceptable for all aspects.

Conjunctions: A conjunction occurs when two or more planets are at the same degrees or within 6° of each other. Planetary conjunctions combine the power of two or more planets working together. For example, Mars conjunct Venus would give sex appeal, while Jupi-

The Aspects

Conjunction 0°

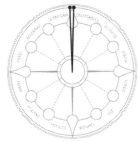

Sextile 60°

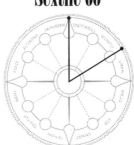

Square 90°

Trine 120°

Opposition 180°

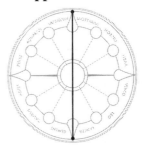

Chart No. 4

ter conjunct Venus would indicate a tendency more toward universal love.

Sextiles: A sextile is two planets at a 60° angle from each other. This is a positive, harmonious aspect. Jupiter sextile Neptune would give an interest in the mystical, while Mars sextile Saturn would indicate that the individual has self-discipline.

Squares: A square is a 90° aspect. It indicates difficulties in the planetary influences and energies involved. Jupiter square Moon would create an exaggerated emotional expression, while Saturn square Moon might create a tendency for depression.

Trines: A trine is a 120° aspect. It is the most positive, free-flowing aspect in astrology. Good things come when people have trine aspects. Uranus trine Mars would give a person tremendous energy, and Venus trine Saturn would indicate artistic ability.

Oppositions: An opposition is a 180° aspect. It is a difficult aspect, similar to the square. In an opposition, planets are on opposite sides of the earth from one another. Sun opposition Moon would indicate a conflict between a person's inner and outer self, whereas Mars opposition Saturn would indicate a tendency toward anger and wrath.

A shorthand way of remembering the aspects is this: 90° and 180° aspects are bad, 60° and 120° aspects are good. When astrologers look at a chart, we look for patterns of planets in these configurations. It is when we see large patterns of planets arranged in good or bad aspects that we see the powerful effects of astrology.

One might ask why 90° and 180° aspects between planets are bad and 60° and 120° aspects between planets are good. Interestingly enough, the answer to this question is contained in the physics of the solar system.

Beginning in the 1940s, RCA began conducting a

research program on the effect of planetary angles on magnetic storms and radio interference on the earth. An RCA engineer by the name of John Nelson found that he could predict magnetic storms on the basis of planetary angles. These angles were the 90° and 180° angles used in astrology for predicting bad aspects. What happens is that planets millions of miles apart can create magnetic field disruptions within the solar system.

The Cayce readings show that these conditions affect the influx of souls into the earth. Souls taking their flight back to earth from planetary sojourns during these time periods have to deal with discordant energies. Likewise, discordant energies would attract discordant souls to return to earth during these storms.

The opposite is also true. When the planetary angles are in more positive aspect, more harmonious souls return to earth.

To illustrate how to identify aspects in an astrological chart, I like to use my own chart as an example because it is very easy to read. (See Chart No. 5.)

As stated earlier, each sign in the chart represents 30° of arc on a circle. The signs move counterclockwise from 0° Aries to 0° Taurus to 0° Gemini, etc. Zero degrees Aries is only 1° away from 29° Pisces, so, with a 6° orb, planets can be conjunct while located in different signs.

The angle between two planets can be determined by counting the number of signs between them. In my chart, Pluto is two signs away from Jupiter, therefore it is 60° away. Jupiter and Pluto are within 6° of each other (26° Gemini and 24° Leo, respectively); therefore, they are close enough to be considered in sextile aspect to each other.

My conjunction of Venus, the Moon, and Neptune in Libra illustrates the different aspects very well. It is

Kirk Nelson
November 4, 1953
1:40 p.m. Atlanta, Ga.

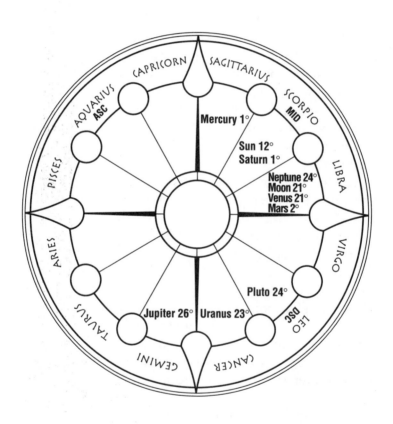

Chart No. 5

60° from Pluto, 90° from Uranus, and 120° from Jupiter. The Jupiter and Pluto aspects to my Libra conjunction are good, but the Uranus aspect is bad.

When planets are close to the cusps of different signs, this can create what is known as a "hidden aspect." In my chart, Jupiter is 120° or in a trine with Saturn, because Saturn in Scorpio is close to the cusp of Libra, and Jupiter in Gemini is close to the cusp of Cancer.

The way astrologers predict future events in a person's life is to superimpose the transiting planets for any time in the future over the planets of the birth chart. A *transiting planet* is simply any position of a planet during the years after the date of birth. These transiting planets effect people in different ways, depending on how they line up with a person's birth-chart planets.

In January 1997, transiting Jupiter was at 25° Capricorn, which is in 90° aspect to my Venus, Moon, Neptune conjunction in Libra. In addition, this transiting Jupiter was in opposition or 180° aspect with my *natal* or *birth-chart* Uranus. This configuration of planets in 90° and 180° aspect is known as a "T-square" and is the worst possible aspect in astrology. It was a very difficult time in my life.

In January 1998, transiting Jupiter was at 25° Aquarius and in trine, or 120° aspect, with my natal or birth-chart Jupiter in Gemini, and my Venus, Moon, Neptune conjunction in Libra. This arrangement of planets, all in 120° aspect with each other, is known as a "grand trine" and is the best possible aspect in astrology. It indicates a positive, harmonious flow of energy. My life during that time was positive and harmonious.

A Note About Astrological Houses

Most astrologers superimpose on their charts a house

structure, which overlaps the signs. There are twelve houses, just as there are twelve signs. The first house cusp is determined by the sign position on the eastern horizon at the time and place of birth. In other words, if you were born at 1:40 p.m., on November 4, 1953, in Atlanta, Georgia, the sign on the eastern horizon would be Aquarius, so your *ascendant* or *rising sign* would be Aquarius. The sign position directly overhead is called the *midheaven*, and the sign position on the western horizon is called the *descendant*. These cusp positions are important because Cayce says that the planet closest to the ascendant or the midheaven is the planet that has the greatest influence on the incoming soul. This is one of the most important facts in our study of astrology. Because of this, I have indicated the ascendant, descendant, and midheaven on the charts in this book with the designations ASC, DSC, and MID.

In his readings, Cayce almost never mentions the houses, and I do not believe they are very important. I have left them out of the charts in this book for that reason, and also to make the astrological charts easier to read for those who are not professional astrologers.

6

Edgar Cayce's Planetary Sojourns

One of the best illustrations of how astrology works is the story of Edgar Cayce and his past lives. The Cayce readings provide intimate details of Cayce's past lives and the planetary sojourns that Cayce himself experienced between lives. By examining his past lives and his planetary sojourns, we can see how our own actions and consciousness play roles in our sojourns in the planetary realms.

The first of Cayce's past lives we want to consider is that of the Egyptian priest Ra Ta.

From the Sun
Ra Ta

Ra Ta was a spiritual leader in ancient Egypt around 10,500 B.C. In that life, he attained a high level of spiritual awareness that led to great psychic ability. When he came to a leadership position in Egypt, he built two spiritual centers, the Temple Beautiful and the Temple of Sacrifice. The Temple Beautiful helped people with their spiritual development, while the Temple of Sacrifice helped people with physical problems, much as a hospital would today.

Ra Ta's greatest achievement was the building of the Great Pyramid and the Sphinx. The Great Pyramid is a temple of initiation, and the Sphinx is the guardian of an ancient repository of knowledge known as the Hall of Records. The construction of these two great monuments was aided by the legendary Hermes, a previous incarnation of Jesus, according to the readings.

Cayce's soul reached such a high level of attunement that when he was born as Ra Ta, he was immaculately conceived. In other words, he was born without an earthly father. When his mother told others in her tribe of this, few believed her. When Ra Ta grew older, however, many changed their minds when they saw what an extraordinary man he was.

Prior to this life as Ra Ta, Cayce's soul had a sojourn in a most unusual planetary realm, the Sun.

> **But the entrance into the Ra-Ta experience, when there was the journeying from materiality—or the being translated in materiality as Ra-Ta—was from the infinity forces, or from the Sun; with those influences that draw upon the planet itself, the earth and all those about same.**
>
> **Is it any wonder that in the ignorance of the earth the activities of that entity were turned into that influence called the sun worshippers? This was because of the abilities of its influences in the experiences of each individual, and the effect upon those things of the earth in nature itself; because of the atmosphere, the forces as they take form from the vapors created even by same; and the very natures or influences upon vegetation!**

> The very natures or influences from the el-
> emental forces themselves were drawn in those
> activities of the elements within the earth, that
> could give off their vibrations because of the in-
> fluences that attracted or draw away from one
> another. This was produced by that which had
> come into the experiences in materiality, or into
> being, as the very nature of water with the sun's
> rays; or the ruler of thy own little solar system,
> thy own little nature in the form ye may see in
> the earth!   5755-1

Ra Ta's great influence on Egypt led to later king-
doms worshiping a Sun god they called "Ra." This
shows not only the influence on Egyptian culture of
Cayce's life as Ra Ta, but also reflects Cayce's planetary
sojourn in the Sun prior to his life as Ra Ta.

After achieving an extremely high level of consciousness as Ra Ta, Cayce's soul experienced a planetary sojourn in that greatest of realms, Arcturus.

From Arcturus
Uhjltd—The Bedouin Leader

Uhjltd was the leader of a tribe of Bedouin warriors
who lived in the desert lands of Persia thousands of
years before the birth of Christ. The tribe he belonged
to survived by raiding the rich caravans that moved
through their territory along the trading routes to the
Far East.

Just like his experience as Ra Ta, Cayce's soul during
the Uhjltd incarnation yearned for a higher calling. He
felt that his tribe could do better if they lived in peace
and learned to cooperate with their neighbors. These
ideals had come from Uhjltd's previous life as Ra Ta and
his subsequent planetary sojourn in Arcturus.

> . . . Uhjltd, was from even without the sphere
> of thine own orb; for the entity came from those
> centers about which thine own solar system
> moves—in Arcturus.
>
> For there had come from those activities, in
> Uhjltd, the knowledge of the oneness, and of
> those forces and powers that would set as it were
> the universality of its relationships, through its
> unity of purpose in all spheres of human experi-
> ence; by the entity becoming how? Not aliens,
> then—not bastards before the Lord—but sons—
> co-heirs with Him in the Father's kingdom.
>
> 5755-1

Uhjltd founded a city based on higher principles and
named the city Is-Shlan-doen. Because of Uhjltd's spiritual leadership, Is-Shlan-doen quickly grew into an important trading center for all the groups in the area.

In the city, Uhjltd lived with his wife and his two sons.
One of his sons was named Zend. According to the
Cayce readings, Zend was a previous incarnation of
Jesus. Zend later grew into greatness and founded the
religion that became Zoroastrianism.

Unfortunately, because Is-Shlan-doen was so successful, neighboring groups became jealous and plotted to
destroy it. They lured Uhjltd and his wife away from
the city, and, in an act of treachery, assassinated them.

This act of deceit caused Cayce's soul to have a mis-
trust of friendships for many lifetimes into the future. It
also caused his soul to become angry and seek vengeance, feelings which led it to a planetary sojourn in
Mars.

From Mars
Xenon—The Trojan Warrior

While the Cayce readings do not specifically say that

Cayce's soul had a sojourn in Mars before his lifetime as Xenon, the Trojan warrior, this would seem to be the case. We are told that after his lifetime as Uhjltd, Cayce's soul sought vengeance. This desire for vengeance was based on Cayce's soul feeling anger at being betrayed and murdered during his lifetime as Uhjltd.

In Troy, Xenon was a Martian figure. He was a soldier who had a considerable temper. Anger and war are two qualities strongly associated with Mars sojourns.

> **For the sojourn in Troy was as the soldier, the carrying out of the order given, with a claim for activities pertaining to world affairs—a spreading . . .**
>
> **Yet the quick return to the earthly sojourn in Troy, and the abuse of these, the turning of these for self—in the activities attempted—brought about the changes that were wrought.   5755-1**

The story of Troy is well known, but Xenon's part in it is not so well known. One of the leaders of Troy eloped with Helen, the wife of the king of Sparta in Greece. The Greeks became infuriated and lay siege to Troy for nine years. Ultimately they tricked the Trojans with the famous Trojan horse. During the final battle, the Trojan warrior, Hector, and the Greek warrior, Achilles, fought a legendary duel and both were killed.

Xenon, Cayce's incarnation during this period, was the gatekeeper of the city of Troy. When the Trojans were tricked by the Greek's wooden horse, Xenon killed himself in shame and humiliation. This led to a feeling of self-doubt for Cayce in many lifetimes to come.

Cayce's soul had fallen far—from the greatness of Ra Ta and a sojourn in Arcturus to the anger and vengeance of a Mars sojourn and the defeat and suicide in Troy.

From Jupiter
Lucius—The Christian Minister

After his life in Troy, Cayce had a planetary sojourn in Jupiter and was reincarnated as Lucius, a leader in the early Christian church. Lucius was one of the seventy disciples appointed by Jesus to be the successors of His ministry. In fact, it was Lucius, not Luke, who wrote the Gospel of Luke, according to the Cayce readings. Lucius's life exemplifies Jupiter's influence as the planet of religion, philosophy, and the universal consciousness.

Before that we find the influence was drawn for a universality of activity from Jupiter; in those experiences of the entity's sojourn or activity as the minister or teacher in Lucius. For the entity gave for the gospel's sake, a love, an activity and a hope through things that had become as of a universal nature.

Yet coming into the Roman influence from the earthly sojourn in Troy, we find that the entity through the Jupiterian environment was trained— as we understand—by being tempered to give self from the very universality, the very bigness of those activities in Jupiter.   5755-1

After the death, resurrection, and ascension of Jesus, Lucius was appointed bishop of the church of Laodicea by John the Beloved. This led to a dispute between Paul and Lucius about whether it was right for Lucius to be married and still serve as the leader of the church. The dispute was smoothed over, and Lucius lived a life of service to the Master, Jesus.

During that lifetime, Lucius, the Cayce soul, befriended the disciple Andrew, who in his twentieth-century life incarnated as Edgar Cayce's son, Hugh Lynn.

From Venus
A Love Child in France

Cayce's next incarnation was as the child of an illicit union between members of the court of the Sun King, Louis XIV of France.

Agatha Beille, one of the daughters of the king, had an affair with James, the Duke of York, who was already engaged to be married. She gave up the child and entered a convent at the age of twenty. The child was subsequently murdered at the age of five to prevent him from ever becoming king.

Cayce describes this lifetime and his Venus sojourn prior to it in the following reading:

> We find that the activity of the same entity in the earthly experience before that, in a French sojourn, followed the entrance into Venus.
>
> What was the life there? How the application?
>
> A child of love! A child of love—the most hopeful of all experiences of any that may come into a material existence; and to some in the earth that most dreaded, that most feared!
>
> (These side remarks become more overburdening than what you are trying to obtain! but you've opened a big subject, haven't you?)
>
> In Venus the body-form is near to that in the three-dimensional plane. For it is what may be said to be rather *all*-inclusive. For it is that ye would call love—which, to be sure, may be licentious, selfish; which also may be so large, so inclusive as to take on the less of self and more of the ideal, more of that which is *giving*.
>
> What is love? Then what is Venus? It is beauty, love, hope, charity—yet all of these have their extremes. But these extremes are not in the ex-

pressive nature or manner as may be found in
the tone or attunement of Uranus; for they (in
Venus) are more in the order that they blend as
one with another.   5755-1

From Scorpio and Venus
John Bainbridge

Edgar Cayce's next incarnation was as John Bainbridge,
a gambling, womanizing wanderer in the frontier days
of America. During that lifetime, Cayce lost in soul development, because John Bainbridge went from place
to place taking advantage of people by cheating them at
cards and having "many escapades that have to do with
those of the nature of the relations with the opposite
sex." (294-8)

Cayce's soul entered the Bainbridge lifetime inexpli-
cably from a sign, Scorpio, with Venus as the second
influence. These influences fit the description of
Bainbridge, since Scorpio is the bad boy of the zodiac,
and Venus is the planet concerned with relationships
and the opposite sex. The problem with Bainbridge was
that he used these relationships for self alone.

> The entity as Bainbridge was born in the Eng-
> lish land under the *sign*, as ye would term, of
> Scorpio; or from Venus as the second influence ...

> So the entity passed through that experience,
> and on entering into materiality abused same; as
> the wastrel who sought those expressions of
> same in the loveliness for self alone, without giv-
> ing—giving of self in return for same.

> Hence we find the influences wielded in the
> sojourn of the entity from the astrological as-
> pects or emotions of the mental nature are the
> ruling, yet must be governed by a standard.

And when self is the standard, it becomes very distorted in materiality.   5755-1

Bainbridge overcame much of the bad karma from his lifetime, when, in the final act of his life, he saved his companions from death while crossing the Ohio River. They had been attacked by Indians, and Bainbridge drowned after helping his friends to safety. This was a very courageous act. As the Bible says, "Greater love hath no man than this, that a man lay down his life for his friends." (John 15:13)

From Uranus
Edgar Cayce

After his life as the wastrel, Bainbridge, Cayce's soul had a planetary sojourn in Uranus and then was born as Edgar Cayce on March 18, 1877, near Hopkinsville, Kentucky.

From an astrological aspect, then, the greater influence at the entrance of this entity that ye call Cayce was from Uranus. Here we find the extremes. The sojourn in Uranus was arrived at from what type of experience or activity of the entity? As Bainbridge, the entity in the material sojourn was a wastrel, one who considered only self; having to know the extremes in the own experience as well as others. Hence the entity was drawn to that environ. Or, how did the Master put it? "As the tree falls, so does it lie." Then in the Uranian sojourn there are the influences from the astrological aspects of *extremes;* and counted in thy own days from the very position of that attunement, that tone, that color. For it is not strange that music, color, vibration, are all a part of the planets, just as the planets are a part— and a pattern—of the whole universe. Hence to

that attunement which it had merited, which it had meted in itself, was the entity drawn for the experience. What form, what shape?

The birth of the entity into Uranus was not from the earth into Uranus, but from those stages of consciousness through which each entity or soul passes. It passes into oblivion as it were, save for its consciousness that there is a way, there is a light, there is an understanding, there have been failures and there are needs for help. Then help *consciously* is sought!

Hence the entity passes along those stages that some have seen as planes, some have seen as steps, some have seen as cycles, and some have experienced as places.

How far? How far is tomorrow to any soul? How far is yesterday from thy consciousness?

You are *in* same (that is, all time as one time), yet become gradually aware of it; passing through, then, as it were, God's record or book of consciousness or of remembrance; for meeting, being measured out as it were to that to which thou hast attained.

Who hath sought? Who hath understood?

Only they that seek shall find!

Then, born in what body? That as befits that plane of consciousness; the *extremes*, as ye would term same.

As to what body—what has thou abused? What hast thou used? What hast thou applied? What has thou neglected in thy extremes, thy extremities?

These are consciousnesses, these are bodies.

5755-1

Uranus reflects the extremes, and, if we look back at Cayce's past lives, they certainly were extreme. The high spiritual achievements of Ra Ta and Uhjltd contrast greatly with the wrath of Xenon and the selfishness of Bainbridge.

The readings told Cayce that the question of which of these extremes would manifest in himself would be answered by his own will:

> **One that will always be either very good or very bad, very wicked or very much given to good works. Ultra in all forces. Very poor, very rich. One scaling to the heights in intellectual ability and capacity, or groveling in the dregs of self-condemnation, influenced at such times by those forces either coming as afflictions from the various phases of developing, from which the entity has received its experience, or controlled by will as exercised in the present sphere.   294-8**

Even though Uranus was the main influence on his life, Cayce had sojourns in other planetary realms as well. This idea of many different planetary sojourns between lifetimes emerges in most of the life readings that Cayce gave. In other words, most people have more than one planetary sojourn between lives. According to the readings, Cayce had sojourns in seven of the eight planets.

> **... from that of Uranus, with the elements of Venus, Neptune, Jupiter and Mercury, with the affliction in Mars and Saturn.   294-19**

It is fascinating to see how each of Cayce's planetary sojourns influenced his twentieth-century life. However, the greatest influence was Uranus, the planet of psychic phenomenon. Cayce, of course, was one of the greatest psychics of all time. The readings themselves

reveal much of the influences of Cayce's other planetary
sojourns; in particular, the influence of Venus.

> **One who finds much in the scope or sphere of
> intrigue in secret love affairs. One given often to
> the conditions that have to do with the affairs of
> the heart, and of those relations that have to do
> with sex.   294-8**

The influence of Mars is shown in Cayce's past tendency for anger and firearms:

> **One ever within the scope or sphere of fire-
> arms, yet just without.   294-8**

Cayce's sojourn in Jupiter reveals itself in his having
developed strength in spiritual forces:

> **One that finds the greater strength in spiritual
> forces and developing.   294-8**

Neptune's influence helped Cayce through the sooth-
ing influence of great waters.

> **One saved spiritually, mentally and financially
> often through a great amount of waters, for it
> was from the beginning, and will be so unto the
> end of time, as time is reckoned from the earth
> plane, for this entity we find was first manifest in
> the earth plane through the waters as was on the
> earth, and above the earth.   294-8**

Cayce's psychic and occult abilities reached their
greatest heights when Jupiter, Uranus, and Neptune
had their greatest influence:

> **One given to make manifest in the present
> plane much of the forces of psychic and occult
> forces, reaching the greater height of developing
> in such plane in those forces when that of Jupi-
> ter, with Uranus and Neptune, come within the**

scope of the Sun's influence upon the earth plane
and forces.

One that will bring, through such manifestations, joy, peace and quiet to the masses and
multitudes through individual efforts.   294-8

Edgar Cayce's Birth Chart

This knowledge of Edgar Cayce's past lives presents
a unique opportunity to study the relationship between
past soul experiences and present astrological birth
charts. Just what do the planetary positions reveal about
past lives and planetary sojourns? In addition to the
foregoing, the Cayce readings provide an important
clue as to which planet the soul took its flight prior to
its birth in the earth:

The strongest force used in the destiny of man
is the Sun first, then the closer planets to the
earth, or those that are coming to ascension at
the time of the birth of the individual . . .

*Q. Are the tendencies of an individual influenced
most by the planets nearer the earth at the time of
the individual's birth?*

A. At, or from that one which is at the zenith
when the individual is in its place or sphere, or as
is seen from that sphere or plane the soul and
spirit took its flight in coming to the earth plane.
For each plane, in its relation to the other, is just
outside, just outside, relativity of force, as we
gather them together.   3744-4

The readings tell us that the strongest influence in
any chart is the Sun position first, followed by the planet
closest to the ascendant (horizon) or the midheaven (zenith). Therefore, the planet the soul most likely took its
flight from is one of these positions.

If there are several planets in the ascendant to midheaven quadrant of the birth chart, then the one closest to the ascendant will probably be the greatest influence. But remember that astrology is an art, not a science.

With this idea in mind, consider the birth chart of Edgar Cayce. (See Chart No. 6.) Interestingly enough, the planet closest to Cayce's ascendant is Uranus. This fits perfectly, since the readings tell us that Cayce's soul took its flight to earth from Uranus. The fact that soul flight comes from the planet closest to the ascendant or midheaven is a valuable lesson to remember as we try to interpret our own birth charts.

What else can be learned by looking at Cayce's chart? Most of his planets are in 60° and 120° aspects. This implies a person who is very constructive and has a very positive energy. In fact, Cayce's chart is one of the most positive I have ever seen. The way he lived his life was reflective of these influences. He was without doubt a great man.

In terms of planetary aspects, Cayce had Mercury conjunct Saturn, an aspect for a disciplined mind and someone who uses speech with precision. It can also indicate a tendency to worry and doubt, a possible carry-over from Cayce's life in Troy as Xenon.

Cayce also has Saturn conjunct Venus. This is an aspect that shows control of the emotions, a virtue Cayce needed in this life after his lifetime as Bainbridge. Venus conjunct Saturn can sometimes lead to the tendency for depression; once again, a possible carry-over from Troy.

Cayce's Moon, Mercury, and Mars are aligned in positive aspect producing a positive, energetic, mental attitude.

Saturn, Mars, and the Moon are aligned in positive

Edgar Cayce
March 18, 1877
3:03 p.m. near Hopkinsville, Ky.

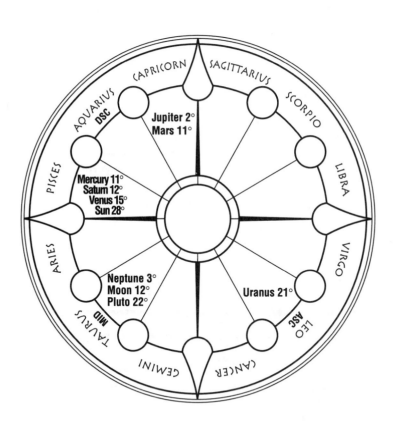

Chart No. 6

aspect, producing an emotional vitality and self-discipline, a pattern brought forward from the Ra Ta, Uhjltd, and Lucius lifetimes.

Venus, Mars, and the Moon are in sextile or trine aspect, showing a tendency for understanding, love, and emotional vitality, as well as an understanding of how to appeal to the opposite sex.

In terms of bad aspects, Cayce's Pisces Sun is in bad aspect with his Capricorn Jupiter. This is an aspect for exaggerated self-expression and extravagance. There are several examples of this in Cayce's life: his attempt to find oil in Texas, the search for Blackbeard's gold in Virginia Beach, and Cayce's hospital, which he lost during the Great Depression.

Cayce's Uranus is in bad aspect with Pluto, and this produces the tendency for extremes and willfulness described in Cayce's own life readings. Uranus on the ascendant also indicates his tremendous psychic ability.

Cayce's Sun is in positive aspect with Pluto, showing an ability to look penetratingly into the deeper mysteries of life. Adding to this is the fact that Cayce's Jupiter is in positive aspect with Neptune, producing mystical awareness and spiritual strength. Cayce was told in his readings that being close to the ocean would help his psychic abilities, and this positive Neptune aspect indicates the help from large bodies of water.

All in all, Cayce's chart reflects the man that he was. It shows his good qualities and his faults, and, combined with our knowledge of his past lives and planetary sojourns, it gives us a great lesson in how astrology works.

7

THE ASTROLOGY OF JESUS

Few people realize that Edgar Cayce gave a date and time for the birth of Jesus: just after midnight on March 19, 4 B.C.

When I first read Cayce's date for Jesus' birth, I was amazed because I had already calculated it for the spring of 4 B.C., using other sources of information based on the appearance of the Star of Bethlehem.

There has been considerable debate through the years about the Star of Bethlehem. Some scholars believe that it was a conjunction of planets, others that it was a comet, and still others that it was merely an apocryphal story.

I always felt, however, that the description of the Star of Bethlehem in the Bible sounded like an exploding star or a supernova.

Supernovas are stars of unusual brilliance and appear suddenly in the sky. This would have alerted the Wise Men or Magi to the birth of Jesus. In fact, the Greek word *magi* means "astrologer" or "one who studies the stars."

Cayce confirms this in a reading in which he was asked how the Magi knew about the birth of Jesus, saying that they knew through the psychic and the astrological.

Confirmation of the supernova theory comes from first-century A.D. Chinese astronomers who were meticulous about reporting new objects that appeared in the sky. This is because the stars were considered to be the emperor's property, and failure to report on changes in the emperor's property would be severely punished. The astronomers reported that a *po hsing*, or "comet without a tail," appeared in the constellation of Aquilla in the spring of 4 B.C. I believe that this *po hsing* was the Star of Bethlehem.

Several other facts push the date of Jesus' birth back to 4 B.C. Most scholars believe that King Herod died in 4 B.C., so the birth of Jesus could not have come any later than 4 B.C., because the Magi visited King Herod before viewing the baby Jesus.

The Bible states that the shepherds were tending their flocks in the fields at night, something that would only happen in the spring or summer, not in the cold of winter.

Cayce describes the Star of Bethlehem poetically in the following reading:

> **Then the entity aided, so that all was in readiness, when in the evening—just before the sun in all its glory of the Palestine hills gave forth almost into the voice of nature, proclaiming the heralding of a new hope, a new birth to the earth, and the glorifying of man's hope, in God—the spectre of His Star in the evening sky brought awe and wonder to all that beheld.**
>
> **And the entity, being anxious, gazed with wondering awe at the *unusual* experience to all, and wept with *joy* of those unfoldments within self, of the emotions that made for the expectancy of**

glory surpassing what had been told of all the glories of her peoples in the days of old . . .

And as soon as its duties were cleared about the home, as the space was very near, the entity started. But as the entity walked into the open upon that Eve, the brightness of His Star came nearer and nearer. And the entity heard, even as the Shepherds, "*Peace* on earth, *good will* to men."   1152-3

As stated earlier, Jesus, like all other souls in the earth, had many lifetimes before His birth in Bethlehem. Cayce tells us that He had past lives as Amilius, Adam, Enoch, Hermes, Melchizedek, Joseph, Joshua, and Jeshua, among others.

Between these lifetimes, the Jesus soul experienced planetary sojourns, although Cayce did not record what they were. However, Ry Redd in his book *Towards a New Astrology* (Inner Vision, 1985) made a listing of possible sojourns based on Jesus' past lives, along with key phrases that describe the soul growth He experienced during them. They are:

1. Amilius from Arcturus: developing through saving others

2. Adam, banished to Saturn: change through separation and death

3. Enoch-Hermes as the Mercurian-Uranian logos: psychic mind of the teacher-prophet

4. Melchizedek as the Neptunian: mysteriously manifested mystic

5. Joseph as the Jupiterian: strength of Israel

6. Joshua as the Martian: wrath of the spiritual warrior

7. Jeshua as the Mercurian: mind of the scribe

8. Jesus as the Venusian: love of the Christ

9. The resurrection as of Pluto: consciousness transcends flesh

The Birth Chart of Jesus

Since we know the time, date, and place of Jesus' birth, we can, through the miracle of computers, calculate Jesus' astrological chart. The result is fascinating. (See Chart No. 7.) Here are the major aspects for Jesus' chart and how they applied to His life:

Sun conjunct Venus. The central ego combined with the planet of love. What could be more appropriate for one whose message was to "love the Lord thy God with all thy heart . . . and thy neighbour as thyself"! (Luke 10:27)

Sun and Venus trine Jupiter. Jupiter gives the broadness of vision and awareness of the universal consciousness and the spiritual side of life. Venus is love, and Jupiter is the universal, so Sun-Venus trine Jupiter gives universal love. Jupiter also represents the masses, and Jesus reached out to the masses throughout His life.

Venus sextile Mars. This aspect gives a balance of the male and female energies. It also gives energy and power to love nature.

Mercury conjunct Saturn. This aspect indicates a very logical, organized mind. People with Mercury conjunct Saturn are precise in their use of speech. What more precise use of speech has there been than the Sermon on the Mount? Mercury conjunct Saturn also gives abilities as an architect or draftsman. In His past as Hermes, Jesus was the architect of the Great Pyramid, and in Palestine He was a carpenter.

Moon trine Mars. This is an aspect for emotional energy and healing, and Jesus used this energy to heal the sick.

Neptune sextile Pluto. This is an aspect for bringing mysticism (Neptune) to the masses (Pluto). It also indicates the Neptunian power over water, as shown

Jesus Christ
March 19, 4 B.C.
just after midnight
Bethlehem, Judea

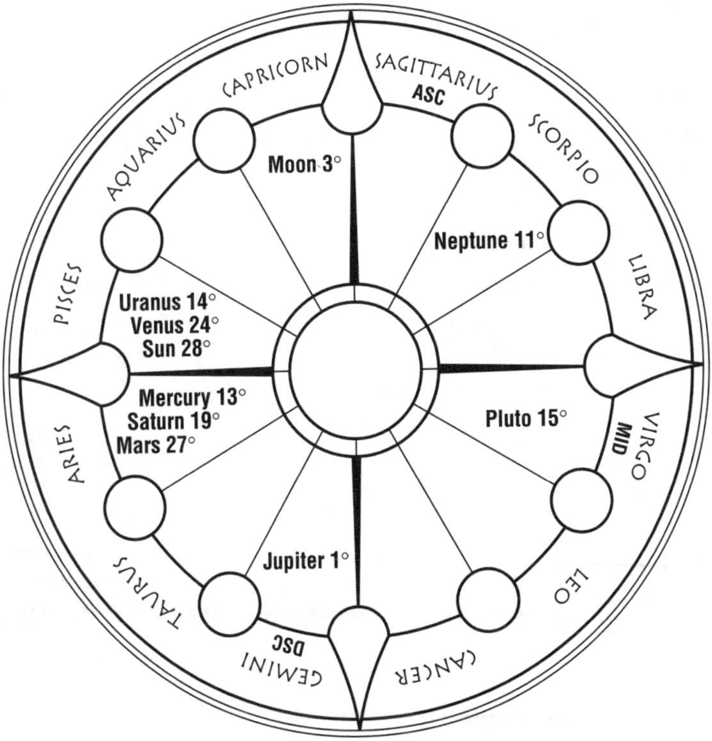

Moon 3°

Neptune 11°

Uranus 14°
Venus 24°
Sun 28°

Mercury 13°
Saturn 19°
Mars 27°

Pluto 15°

Jupiter 1°

ASC

MID

DSC

CAPRICORN SAGITTARIUS SCORPIO LIBRA VIRGO LEO CANCER GEMINI TAURUS ARIES PISCES AQUARIUS

Chart No. 7

when Jesus calmed the storm on the Sea of Galilee.

Uranus trine Neptune. The ultimate psychic-mystic aspect. It is indicative of tremendous spiritual development and psychic ability.

Uranus opposition Pluto. This aspect shows an inner conflict between the extremes of the will. When Jesus was tested by the devil in the wilderness, He had to use His will to overcome temptation. People with this aspect also have difficulty gaining popular acceptance of their ideas.

Sun square Moon. This is an aspect for a conflict between the inner emotions and the outer self. The emotional conflict within Jesus was shown in the Garden of Gethsemane, when He prayed, " . . . let this cup pass from me." (Matthew 26:39) Cayce says this was the greatest test Jesus faced—whether or not to allow Himself to be crucified.

Pluto conjunct midheaven. Pluto, the planet of death and regeneration, on the midheaven symbolizes Jesus' fulfillment in overcoming death through the crucifixion and the resurrection.

Arcturus on the midheaven. The most amazing and esoteric aspect in Jesus' birth chart is that He has Arcturus directly on His midheaven. Cayce said that when a soul had achieved perfection in the earth, it went to Arcturus to move on to other systems or to return to earth to help. Because Jesus had Arcturus on the midheaven, His soul undoubtedly took its flight from the star, Arcturus. This would be exactly what one would expect of a perfected soul.

The Transiting Aspects for Jesus' Ministry

Armed with the knowledge of Jesus' birth-chart planetary positions, we can look at the astrological aspects for different events in His life as well as the influence of the transiting planets.

In researching the events in the life of Jesus, I believe I have determined the dates, times, and astrological aspects for the wedding at Cana, the crucifixion, and the resurrection (see Chart Nos. 8, 9, and 10). The dates and times of the crucifixion and the resurrection are fairly well established through historical sources. The date for the wedding at Cana, however, comes from the Edgar Cayce readings.

In the following reading Cayce gives a poetic description of the wedding at Cana:

> A great deal of that leading to the experience [wine miracle], to be sure, is being skipped over. For, that came about soon after the return of the Master from the Jordan, and His dwelling by the sea, His conversation with Peter—after Andrew had told Peter of the happenings at the Jordan; and there was the wedding in Cana of Galilee.
>
> The girl was a relative of those close to the Mother of Jesus, who prepared the wedding feast—as was the custom in that period, and is yet among those of the Jewish faith who adhere to the traditions as well as custom of those people chosen as the channel because of their purpose with God.
>
> The girl [Clana, 609] to be wed was a daughter of the cousin of Mary, a daughter of a younger sister of Elizabeth, whose name was also Mary. And she was the one spoken of as "the other Mary," and not as some have supposed.
>
> The customs required that there be a feast, which was composed of the roasted lamb with the herbs, the breads that had been prepared in the special ways as were the custom and tradi-

tion of those who followed close to the faith in Moses' law, Moses' custom, Moses' ordinances.

The families of Mary were present, as well as those of the groom.

The groom, in the name Roael, was among the sons of Zebedee; being an elder brother of James and John who later became the close friends and the closer followers of Jesus.

The Master, returning with those who were hangers-on, naturally sought to speak with His mother. Learning of this happening He, too, with the followers, were bid to remain at the feast.

Much wine also was part of the custom. The day was what ye would call June third. There were plenty of flowers and things of the field, yet only a part of those things needed. For, the custom called for more of the meats prepared with certain herbs, and wines.

The day had been fine; the evening was fair, the moon was full. This then brought the activities with the imbibing more and more of wine, more hilarity, and the dance—which was in the form of the circles that were a part of the customs, not only of that land then but that are in your own land now and then being revived.

With those activities, as indicated, the wine ran low. Remember, the sons of Zebedee were among those of the upper class, as would be termed; not the poorer ones. Thence the reason why Mary served or prepared for her relative the feast.

From those happenings that were a portion of her experience upon their return from Egypt— as to how the increase had come in the food when they had been turned aside as they journeyed back towards the Promised Land—Mary felt, knew, was convinced within herself that here

again there might be such an experience, with
her son returning as a man starting upon His
mission. For, what was the pronouncement to
the mother when Gabriel spoke to her? What
was the happening with Elizabeth when the
mother spoke to her?

This might be called a first period of test. For,
had He not just ten days ago sent Satan away,
and received ministry from the angels? This had
come to be known as hearsay. Hence the natural
questioning of the mother-love for the purposes;
this son—strange in many ways had chosen, by
the dwelling in the wilderness for the forty days,
and then the returning to the lowly people, the
fishermen, about this country. It brought on the
questioning by the mother.   5749-15

Cayce says that the date for the wedding at Cana was
June 3. (See Chart No. 8.) He also says that the Moon
was full. Since Jesus' ministry only lasted three years, all
we have to do is look back three or four years from the
time of the crucifixion and find a time when the Moon
was full on June 3. Then we have the date of the wedding at Cana. Astrological tables show that the moon
was full on June 3, A.D. 27, just as Cayce said. This
shows the amazing psychic ability of Edgar Cayce: that
he could look back through time and tell us the exact
date of an event two thousand years ago.

The transiting planetary positions for June 3, A.D.
27, fit perfectly with the event when you compare them
with Jesus' birth chart. Venus, Uranus, Neptune, and
the Moon are aligned in positive aspect with Jesus' natal Sun. The transiting Moon in Scorpio, the transiting
Uranus in Cancer, and Jesus' natal Pisces Sun form a
grand trine in the *water* signs! This aspect fits a miracle
that involves turning water into wine. What a profound

The Wedding at Cana
June 3, A.D. 27
9:00 p.m.
The Grand Trine in the Water Signs

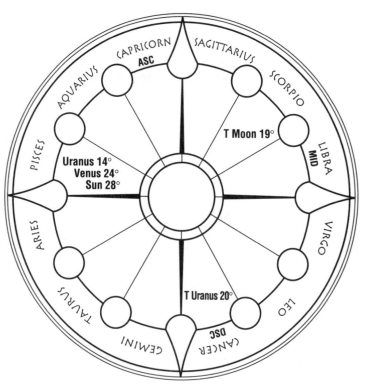

T = Transiting Planets

Chart No. 8

connection between the planetary positions and the event!

This was the first event in Jesus' three-year ministry. One telling fact is that during Jesus' entire ministry Uranus and Neptune were lined up with Jesus' natal Sun. This is because Uranus and Neptune move very slowly from one sign to the next. Uranus is the psychic, and Neptune is the mystic. Jesus' ministry was full of psychic and mystic events.

The Neptune aspect is particularly interesting because of Neptune's connection as the water planet. Jesus was baptized in water; He walked on water; and He changed water into wine. I believe Jesus chose this time period for His ministry, knowing that the aspects were favorable. In fact, Cayce does tell us that Jesus studied astrology.

The Astrology of the Crucifixion

It is generally agreed that Jesus was crucified in A.D. 30. We can determine the day in A.D. 30, because we are told in the Bible that Jesus was crucified during the celebration of the Jewish holiday, Passover. The Jewish calendar is lunar, so by looking at the Moon positions in A.D. 30, we can determine that Jesus was crucified on April 7, A.D. 30. According to the Bible, He died at three o'clock in the afternoon.

The astrological chart for that time and day show some interesting aspects. (See Chart No. 9.) At three o'clock, April 7, A.D. 30, Saturn, the grim reaper, was directly on the midheaven in Jesus' chart. Saturn is in opposition to Pluto, the planet of death and regeneration. When this opposition is matched up with Jesus' birth chart, it produces a grand square, one of the worst aspects in all of astrology. A grand square produces a diffusion of energy. The transiting Saturn-Pluto oppo-

The Crucifixion
April 7, A.D. 30
3:00 p.m. Jerusalem, Israel
The Midheaven T-Square

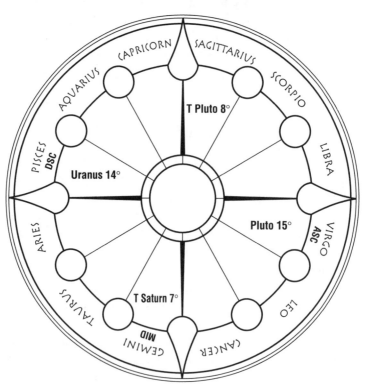

T = Transiting Planets

Chart No. 9

sition combines with Jesus' natal Uranus-Pluto opposition to make the grand square. This grand square combines Uranus (extremes) with Saturn (change) and Pluto (death and regeneration). It is a perfect arrangement for change through death. It is a configuration that would perfectly accompany the crucifixion. This match between Jesus' birth chart with the planets that were transiting in the sky during the crucifixion lends validity to Cayce's date for the birth of Jesus.

The Astrology of the Resurrection

The date of the resurrection is easy to determine once the date for the crucifixion is known. The time I have chosen is 6 a.m., April 9, A.D. 30.

As was the case with the chart for the crucifixion, the chart for the resurrection matches the event very well. (See Chart No. 10.) Most noticeable is that Neptune is directly on Jesus' midheaven. Neptune, the planet of mysticism, is sextile Jupiter, the planet of universal consciousness.

This Jupiter-Neptune sextile is aligned with Jesus' natal Sun in Pisces. His natal Sun is conjunct the transiting Jupiter in Pisces and sextile the transiting Neptune in Capricorn. Jupiter and Neptune are both expansive, mystical, and spiritual planets, and the resurrection can be considered the most spiritual event in human history.

The time of day is also worth noting, since dawn is the beginning of a new day, and Jesus' resurrection meant a new day for all humankind.

Jesus' natal Sun represents the ego, and it is conjunct transiting Jupiter. This produces an awareness of the universal consciousness. Jesus' soul returned from the universal consciousness to reoccupy His body in the tomb, and the stone was rolled away.

The Resurrection
April 9, A.D. 30
6:00 a.m. Jerusalem, Israel
The Midheaven Neptune Sextiles

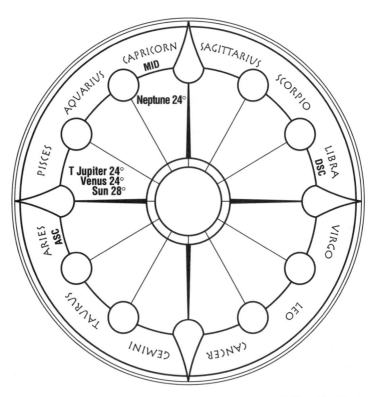

T = Transiting Planets

Chart No. 10

8

THE ASTROLOGY OF PRESIDENTS AND NATIONS

This section will examine the astrological charts of three U.S. presidents. There is a great advantage in examining presidential charts, because the events in their lives are well known, and their personalities have been analyzed to the nth degree.

John F. Kennedy

The birth chart of John F. Kennedy will be considered first. (See Chart No. 11.) It is especially fascinating in that it clearly reveals the aspects for his success, as well as for his untimely death.

Mercury conjunct Mars. People with Mercury conjunct Mars have a great deal of mental energy and love politics and debate. They are direct in their speech and decisive in the decision-making process. This decisiveness was shown in 1960 during the Cuban missile crisis when President Kennedy told the world that "any attack launched from Cuba, on any nation in the West-

John F. Kennedy
May 29, 1917
3:00 p.m. Brookline, Mass.

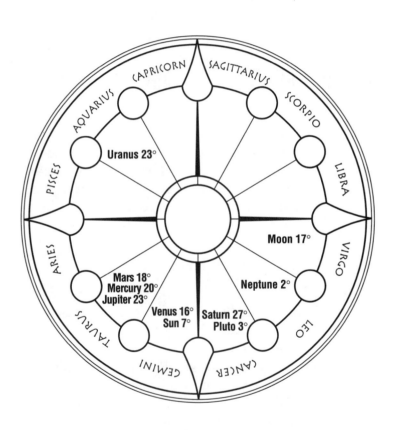

Chart No. 11

ern Hemisphere, will be considered an attack from the Soviet Union on the United States and shall require a full retaliatory response upon the Soviet Union." This is an example of plain speaking, indeed.

Mercury conjunct Jupiter. This is an aspect for intellectual ability and broadness of vision. It gives an ability for speechmaking, and John Kennedy is considered one of the greatest speakers in U.S. history. Kennedy's broad vision can be seen in his political stances on issues such as the Nuclear Test Ban Treaty, the minimum wage bill, the space program, and civil rights.

Mars conjunct Jupiter. This aspect confers energy and enthusiasm. Kennedy was a tireless campaigner, being on the road almost 300 days a year when he ran for president in 1960.

Mercury conjunct Mars and Jupiter. This shows that Kennedy was a bright, motivated, and energetic man. Interestingly, Richard Nixon also had Mercury, Mars, and Jupiter conjunct.

Sun conjunct Venus. This is an aspect for cheerfulness and a love of life. It can produce a love of the arts and a pleasing personality. Kennedy's sense of humor was legendary, and he always seemed to be able to turn a situation around by making fun of himself.

Sun sextile Neptune. People with this aspect tend to be visionaries. They respond to subtle energies that only they can feel. Neptune rules the oceans, and Kennedy's love of sailing and the ocean is well documented.

Moon trine Jupiter. The Moon with Jupiter produces an expansive, generous spirit. This is also an aspect for wealth through inheritance, which clearly came through in John Kennedy's case.

Jupiter sextile Saturn. This aspect produces serious, dignified, even-tempered people. It is an aspect for being able to coordinate large-scale projects that entail heavy responsibilities. It is also an aspect for being involved with politics and the law. John Kennedy exhibited all of these characteristics.

Moon sextile Saturn.   Another aspect for discipline and emotional control, this shows Kennedy's cool demeanor which added much to his ability as a leader.

Mercury square Uranus.   This is an aspect for intellectual conceit and the extremes. People with this aspect can think they are smarter than they are. Uranus is the extremes and Mercury the mind, so people with this aspect might tend to be too mental.

Jupiter square Uranus.   Jupiter square Uranus can indicate a tendency to go off on grandiose ill-defined schemes. The ill-fated invasion of Cuba at the Bay of Pigs can serve as an example. This unsuccessful invasion of Cuba was without a doubt the greatest mistake of Kennedy's presidency.

Mars square Uranus.   This is the assassination aspect. It is an aspect for people who crave danger and take unnecessary risks. It is also the ultimate aspect for a violent death. John Kennedy, Anwar Sadat, and Princess Diana all had this aspect prominently in their charts when they were killed.

The Astrology of the Kennedy Assassination

The transiting aspects for John Kennedy on the day he was killed indicate an uncommon potential for violence. (See Chart No. 12.) Transiting Saturn and the Moon conjunct Kennedy's natal Uranus and square his natal Mars, Mercury, and Jupiter. Transiting Neptune forms a violent T-square with six other planets.

There was another violent T-square at the same time

The Kennedy Assassination
November 22, 1963
12:30 p.m. Dallas, Texas
T-Square

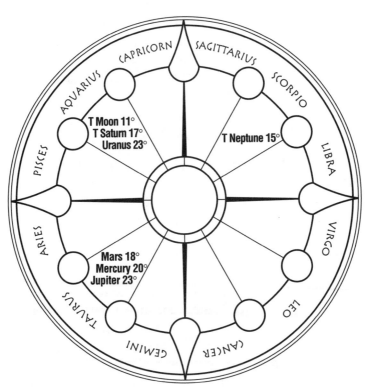

T = Transiting Planets

Chart No. 12

involving transiting Mars and Mercury in Sagittarius, transiting Pluto and Uranus in Virgo, all aligned with Kennedy's natal Sun and Venus in Gemini and natal Moon in Virgo. Seven planets lined up in a second violent T-square.

From an astrological point of view, to have thirteen transiting and natal planets lined up in two different violent T-squares is very rare.

Cayce said that the planet with the greatest influence is the planet nearest the ascendant or midheaven. On November 22, 1963, at 12:30 p.m., in Dallas, Texas, the planet on Kennedy's midheaven was Mars, the planet of anger and violence. If Kennedy had had an astrologer, he could have been forewarned about the danger that awaited him that day.

The Astrology of Ronald Reagan

Ronald Reagan is the only U.S. president to have officially acknowledged using astrology in planning his life, so it would seem appropriate to look at his astrological chart.

When he was sworn in as governor of California, he insisted that the ceremony take place just before midnight. This must have been a time chosen for its positive astrological aspects. Later, when he became president, his wife, Nancy, consulted her personal astrologer to plan his press conferences and travels to foreign countries. Reagan was called the "Teflon president" because the press could never make any charges or accusations stick to him. Undoubtedly, his use of astrology in planning press conferences was one of the things that helped keep him out of trouble.

Reagan's astrological chart has aspects that reflect his virtues as well as his faults. The transiting planets over the last twenty years show the various stages of his life. (See Chart No. 13.)

Mercury conjunct Uranus. This aspect indicates someone with a brilliant mind. Reagan's lightening quick wit showed often during his presidency. Uranus rules television and electronics, and Reagan was a master at going over the heads of the press directly to the American people by using television. Uranus also rules astrology, and having the planet of the mind conjunct the planet of astrology shows that Reagan understood the subject.

Mars sextile Venus. Mars and Venus together give sexual attraction and a harmony between the masculine and feminine selves. Reagan was a matinee idol in his early years as an actor, and this reflects that appeal. People with this aspect also tend to be outgoing and have a lively personality. His personal appeal was a key part of his leadership ability.

Moon sextile Neptune. This aspect gives a keen emotional sensitivity to other people. Since Reagan's Neptune in Cancer is directly conjunct his wife Nancy's Sun, this aspect gives a great emotional-psychic connection between them. There is celestial music between them that only they can hear.

Sun square Moon. Sun square Moon can indicate a conflict between the inner and outer self, sometimes related to a difficult early childhood. Reagan's father was an alcoholic, and he often had to take care of things at an early age. Adult children of alcoholics have certain personality traits in common, such as trying to pretend problems do not exist, rather than facing them directly.

Sun square Jupiter. This is an aspect for doing too much too fast and having exaggerated self-expression. Reagan placed the country hundreds of billions of dollars in debt to defend against an adversary, the Soviet

Ronald Reagan
February 6, 1911
(time unknown)
Tampico, Illinois

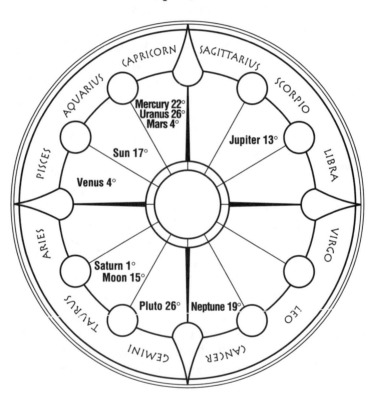

Chart No. 13

Union, which in the long run was not as strong as had been believed.

Saturn square Uranus.   Extreme change is the best description of this aspect. People with this aspect have a conflict between their radical and conservative selves. In his early years, Reagan was a liberal Democrat, but when he got older, he switched to being a conservative Republican. This aspect can also lead to dictatorial tendencies, and Reagan's firing of 10,000 air traffic controllers is an example of that. In the late 1980s transiting Pluto affected this square, and it was a difficult time for him. He eventually left the presidency and later developed Alzheimer's disease.

Moon trine Mercury.   People with this aspect are very good at communicating their emotions. They are fluent in speech and have a good deal of common sense. Reagan was known as the "Great Communicator" during his presidency, so this seems to fit.

Sun trine Pluto.   This configuration gives power and self-awareness. People with this aspect have penetrating insight and the ability to cut to the root of any problem. These people see things as they are. When Reagan called the Soviet Union an "evil empire," he was severely criticized as being too conservative politically. The problem with this criticism is that, in my opinion, the Soviet Union was an evil empire and that Reagan spoke the truth.

This Sun-Pluto aspect in Reagan's chart is interesting because almost every president elected in the last forty years has had a positive natal Sun-transiting-Pluto relationship. Pluto gives power and popularity.

During the 1980s, transiting Pluto was in Libra, setting up a grand trine with Reagan's natal Aquarius Sun trine Gemini Pluto. (See Chart No. 14.) He was reelected in a huge landslide with his "It's morning in

1982
Transiting Grand Trine for Ronald Reagan

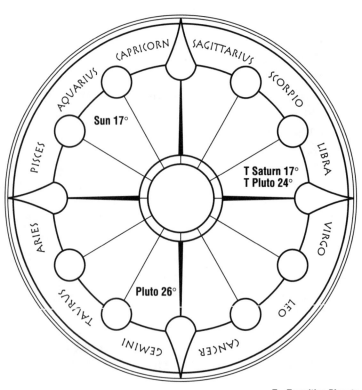

T = Transiting Planets

Chart No. 14

America" approach. This transiting aspect is a good example of how the outer planets work.

Because Uranus, Neptune, and Pluto move so slowly, they are only aligned with a person's natal Sun once or twice during his or her lifetime. It is during these times when a person's Sun is aligned with transiting Uranus, Neptune, and Pluto that whatever he or she has built comes to fruition. The outer planets represent a kind of destiny in our lives. Reagan spent his whole political career working for what happened to him in the 1980s. Having transiting Neptune and Pluto aligned with his natal Sun helped him with his success.

Mars trine Saturn.   This is an aspect for strong discipline and tremendous willpower and ambition. A strong Saturn is typical for someone with the guts to run for president. This is also an aspect for military involvements, and Reagan's interest in a strong defense establishment is shown.

Jupiter trine Neptune.   This is an aspect for mystical awareness and a boundless imagination. It is also an aspect that influences Ronald Reagan's relationship with Nancy because his Neptune is conjunct her Sun. It strengthens the bond between them with the sensitivity of Neptune and the optimism of Jupiter.

Mercury opposition Neptune.   This configuration can indicate mental confusion and deceit. One of Reagan's characteristics was that of telling great-sounding stories which, when checked against the facts, turned out not to be true. *Time* magazine once took several stories that Reagan told at a press conference and checked them out. They all turned out to be not quite true. People with this aspect are not deliberately deceitful; they just color things from their own perspective.

The dark side of this aspect came into play for Reagan

in the 1990s, when transiting Uranus and Neptune went into Capricorn, accentuating his natal Mercury-Neptune opposition. The mental confusion aspect manifested itself in the form of Alzheimer's disease. This is a good example of how the outer planets influence our lives. In the 1980s the outer planets were in Reagan's favor, and he was riding high as president. Then, in the 1990s, the planets swung around and were in bad aspect, and Reagan experienced serious problems with his health.

There was one period in the 1980s, when Reagan had some particularly bad outer planet aspects. During the worst of this period, he disappeared for about six weeks—not holding any press conferences or public appearances. It occurred during the worst of the Iran-Contra scandal, when it seemed as if he might be in real trouble politically. His astrologer must have told him to lie low during this time period and reappear when the aspects were better. He waited until the aspects improved, and when he came back before the public during a time of good aspects, it was as if the scandal had never happened. It was a brilliant combination of political and astrological strategies. The Teflon president had done it again.

The Astrology of Richard M. Nixon

Few figures in the twentieth century are as intriguing or as tragic as Richard M. Nixon. He was elected president in one of the largest landslide victories in American history, and then, two years later, he was forced to resign in disgrace. Nixon's astrological chart shows the intelligence and drive that brought him to the top, as well as the dictatorial and deceitful nature that brought him down. (See Chart No. 15.)

Richard Nixon
January 9, 1913
9:14 p.m. Yorba Linda, Calif.

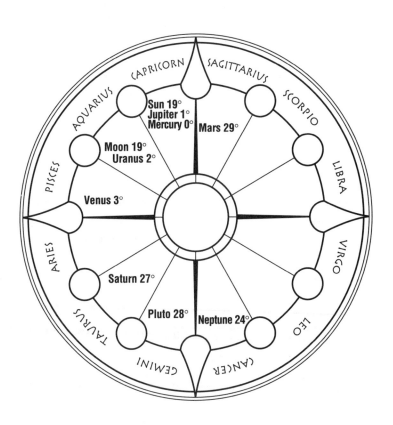

Chart No. 15

Mercury conjunct Mars. This aspect gives an energetic mind and a keen intellect. It is also an aspect for a love of debate and politics. Nixon's debates with John Kennedy are examples of this and, more so, maybe even Nixon's debate with then Soviet premier Nikita Khrushchev when Nixon was vice president. This was called the "kitchen debate," because it took place at an exhibition of American consumer products in Moscow.

Mercury conjunct Jupiter. This is another aspect that indicates a good mind. It gives broadmindedness and vision, particularly in any field dealing with foreign countries. Nixon was adept in foreign affairs—negotiating nuclear arms treaties with the Soviet Union. His greatest foreign policy triumph was the opening of relations with China. Nixon's diplomatic initiative to China showed that he had broad vision with respect to foreign affairs.

Mars conjunct Jupiter. This configuration gives great energy and strength. As with the other presidents whose charts are examined here, this aspect reflects a powerful drive and ambition. It is also an aspect for patriotism and military involvement. Nixon, like Reagan, was in favor of a strong military.

Mercury sextile Venus. Having Venus and Mercury together helps with communication and mental ability. Nixon's Venus was in Pisces; and his wife, Pat, was a Pisces. This Mercury aspect helped the mental connection between them.

Mars sextile Venus. Here is an aspect for the balance of male and female energies. Venus, the planet of love, is aligned with Pat's Sun, and his Mars gives energy and attraction to their relationship.

Venus sextile Jupiter. Venus love combines with the bigness of Jupiter. Once again, the love aspects in Nixon's chart reflect his love for his wife. Jupiter rules foreign affairs, so this aspect can also indicate a love of diplomacy.

Saturn sextile Neptune. This arrangement indicates the ability to plan and successfully carry out projects in secret. It gives the depth of awareness needed for subtle strategy. It also contributes to organizational ability. The Neptune aspect involves large bodies of water, and Nixon, like Kennedy, enjoyed the ocean.

Moon trine Pluto. The planet of the will with the planet of emotions gives intense emotions and will-power. There is no doubt that Nixon was an intense and willful man who sought to control himself and his emotions, especially before the public.

Saturn trine Uranus. This aspect shows a genius for organizational ability. Nixon produced such a well-oiled political machine that the Democrats were trounced when Nixon ran for reelection in 1972. But like a hero in a Greek tragedy, he had a character flaw that ultimately led to his downfall.

Mars opposition Pluto. These two planets in bad aspect can be characterized as "my way or no way"— the planet of will with the planet of anger. People with this aspect make vehement enemies. Nixon was so determined to fight his opponents that he had his staff compose an "enemies list" of people who opposed his policies.

Mercury opposition Pluto. This is an aspect for people who are mentally domineering and abrupt or harsh in speech. The tape recordings Nixon made at the White House of his meetings with aides showed his blunt, harsh speech. Another good example of this aspect is that, at the end of his failed 1962 California gubernatorial campaign, Nixon lashed out at the press by saying, "This is my last press conference. You won't have Dick Nixon to kick around anymore!"

Jupiter opposition Pluto. Like all the above-mentioned Pluto aspects, this aspect can indicate dictatorial tendencies. It shows an autocratic nature and domineering attitude. This is the side of Nixon that was dogmatic about his own philosophy above all others. This aspect also manifests in the desire for great power.

There are two key aspects that seem to epitomize Richard Nixon: Sun trine Saturn and Sun opposition Neptune.

Sun trine Saturn. This is an aspect for a serious, practical, hard-working person. These are the "old souls" who seem old even when they are young. It gives good organizational ability and self-discipline. Cayce says that Saturn represents change, and one of the things that Nixon did after his defeat in 1962 was to create a new image for himself: the so-called "New Nixon." He forced himself to change through hard work.

Sun opposition Neptune. This is an aspect for self-deception and self-delusion. People with this aspect see things through the colored glass of their own biases. They see themselves as inspired leaders, but this belief is based on their own desire for self-importance. This is the "Tricky Dick" side of Richard Nixon. He wanted to be remembered in posterity, so he taped all his meetings in the White House. But these tapes caught him in a lie, and he was forced to resign. Now he will be remembered by posterity as the only president to resign in disgrace. The classic moment came at a press conference during the height of the Watergate scandal when he said, "I am not a crook."

The transiting outer-planet aspects during the 1960s and the '70s reflected Nixon's rise and fall. In 1968, all the outer planets were aligned with Nixon's Sun. Transiting Uranus, Neptune, and Pluto were all in positive aspect with Nixon's natal Sun—the classic destiny aspect described earlier. Then in the '70s it all began to change. Uranus and Pluto both went into Libra (see Chart No. 16) and, by 1974, were in bad aspect with Nixon's natal Sun in Capricorn. These aspects show not only what happened to Nixon, but how it was his own behavior and egotism that brought about his fall. Having two transiting outer planets in Libra set up a T-square with Nixon's natal Sun-Neptune opposition—the "Tricky Dick" aspect we mentioned earlier. When the outer planets are with you, things flow and you are in tune. When they are against you, you must use your will to overcome what Cayce called the urges, inclinations, and tendencies that are the influence of astrology.

The Astrology of the United States of America

What kind of country is the United States of America? What are its strengths and weaknesses? As Americans, it is difficult to see ourselves as the rest of the world sees us, but through the use of astrology we can gain a glimpse into the personality of the United States.

The U.S. was born on July 4, 1776, in Philadelphia, Pennsylvania, with the signing of the Declaration of Independence. A look at the positions of the planets on that date shows some very interesting aspects. (See Chart No. 17.)

Sun conjunct Jupiter. The central ego (Sun) conjunct the planet of broadmindedness and the universal consciousness. This aspect tends to make the United States an expansive, magnanimous, and optimistic nation. This is also an aspect for spiritual awareness and freedom. A higher percentage of Americans attend church than the citizens of any other country in the

1974
Transiting T-Square for Richard Nixon

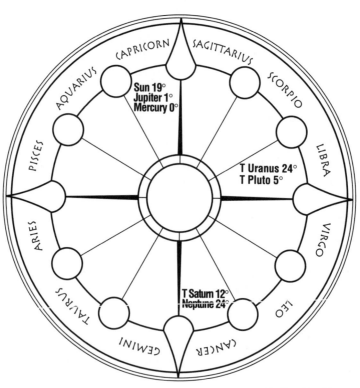

T = Transiting Planets

Chart No. 16

The United States of America
July 4, 1776
Philadelphia, Pa.

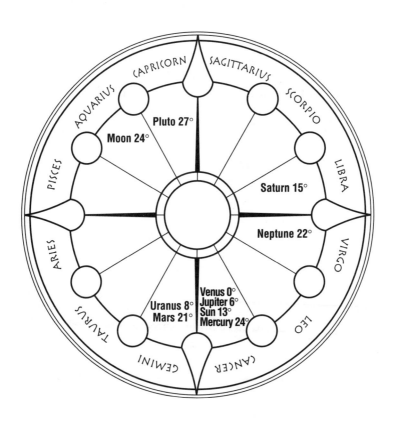

Pluto 27°

Moon 24°

Saturn 15°

Neptune 22°

Venus 0°
Uranus 8°   Jupiter 6°
Mars 21°   Sun 13°
Mercury 24°

Chart No. 17

world. The American ideal of freedom and democracy has spread all over the world in the last century.

Venus conjunct Jupiter. This is an aspect for a happy and positive disposition. Artistic ability is also suggested by this aspect, and many musicians, artists, and performers from around the world have emigrated to the U.S. for greater artistic freedom.

Sun square Saturn. This is one of the most difficult aspects, as it can indicate a life of drudgery. It reflects the heavy burden of responsibility placed on the United States as the leader of the world. Whenever trouble arises around the world, people look to the U.S. to provide leadership and material aid.

Sun sextile Neptune. This is primarily an aspect for mystical and intuitive awareness. Many of the founding fathers of the United States were members of that mystical brotherhood, the Masons. The eye in the pyramid on the back of the dollar bill is one of the country's most mystical symbols.

Mercury sextile Neptune. This configuration gives an intuitive mind and the ability to carry out plans in secret. It also enhances the imagination artistically. Neptune rules the movies, and the motion picture industry in the U.S. is the best in the world.

Mars square Neptune. This aspect can take the form of alcoholism, drug addiction, or sexual excess. We all recognize these as problems in our society. In addition, any Mars square can cause a nation to be too militaristic. Mars, the god of war, square Neptune, which rules oceans or large bodies of water, can indicate frequent use of its navy in war. In the U.S. we even have a name for this: we call it "gunboat diplomacy."

Moon trine Mars. Moon trine Mars gives emotional intensity and positive feeling. A nation with this aspect will fight for what is right.

Mars trine Saturn. This is the most positive military aspect. It shows the tendency of the U.S. to fight for the freedom and dignity of people around the world. For many years people have looked to the U.S. to deal with the bullies of the world.

Moon trine Saturn. This aspect provides common sense and dignity in carrying out responsibilities. Emotional control is also part of this aspect. The U.S. usually responds to challenges in a conservative, controlled manner.

Neptune trine Pluto. Neptune trine Pluto is an aspect for the positive projection of sea power. The United States has tremendous ocean access with deep-water ports on two oceans, the Atlantic and the Pacific. This helps our economy through shipping and helps our navy as well. Many countries envy our access to warm-water ports.

Saturn trine Uranus. This aspect has to do with science and technology. The U.S. is the world leader in the field of science, and U.S. scientists have won more Nobel Prizes than scientists from any other country. The United States also leads the world in the field of computers, one of the most critical elements of scientific research. Uranus also rules television and aviation, and the U.S. is the world's leader in these fields as well. This Saturn trine Uranus aspect of the American character is reflected in the phrase "American ingenuity."

Mercury opposition Pluto. This is an aspect that indicates mental domineering. Certainly we in the U.S. think we always have the best ideas, but it is important for us not to impose our ideas and culture on the rest of the world. This is a common complaint about the United States by people in foreign countries.

Transiting Aspects for the U.S.

In the natal chart of the United States, the Sun and three planets are in Cancer. The history of the U.S. can be understood by looking at how transiting planets aspect these Cancer planets in the chart at a given point in time. Take, for instance, the last forty years or so. In the early 1960s transiting Pluto in Scorpio, Uranus in Virgo, and Neptune in Virgo were in extremely good aspect with respect to these Cancer planets. At that time, the United States was going through a period of very low unemployment and low inflation. Conditions were so good in the country that the press dubbed the White House "Camelot."

Then, in the late 1960s, Pluto and Uranus moved deeper into Virgo and into a square aspect with the U.S. natal Mars in Gemini. This is a very warlike, violent, dominating aspect, and the United States was torn apart by the political assassinations of Robert Kennedy and Martin Luther King, Jr., and the Vietnam War and the protests against it.

In the 1970s, Pluto moved into Libra and set off the U.S. natal Sun-square-Saturn aspect. (See Chart No. 18.) Cayce says that Saturn represents change, and the U.S. went through an intense period of change during the '70s. We endured the Watergate scandal and the excruciating process of removing a president from office. We also had an economic recession and the Arab oil embargo. In the late '70s, we had a Libra president, Jimmy Carter, announcing that there was a feeling of "malaise" in the country.

It is interesting from an astrological point of view that during this difficult time in the '70s, we had three presidents whose natal Sun positions badly aspected the U.S. natal Sun square Saturn. Capricorns (Nixon), Cancers

1974
Transiting T-Square for the United States

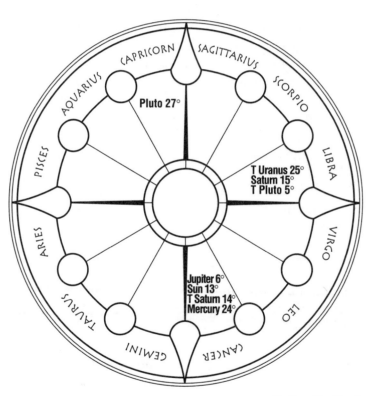

T = Transiting Planets

Chart No. 18

(Ford), and Libras (Carter) do not make good presidents, at least according to astrological analysis. The best Sun positions for U.S. presidents are Aquarius (Franklin Roosevelt, Ronald Reagan) and Scorpio (Teddy Roosevelt).

In the mid-1980s, Pluto in Scorpio swung into trine aspect with the U.S. natal Cancer planets, and, as a result, the U.S.'s self-image became bright. There was an oil glut instead of an oil crisis and a booming economic expansion. It truly was "morning in America."

At the end of the 1990s, Uranus and Neptune moved into Aquarius, signaling the beginning of the Aquarian Age. This created a grand trine in the U.S. natal chart, the best of all possible aspects. This will be the fulfillment of the United States' ultimate destiny, to lead the world into the Age of Aquarius. It is a similar situation astrologically to the end of World War II, when the U.S., as the leader of the free world, extended a hand to help her former enemies, Germany and Japan. But unlike the end of World War II, at the beginning of the Aguarian Age the world will be united in peace and kinship.

The Astrology of the Soviet Union

Another interesting case history in the astrology of nations is the Soviet Union. Even though the Soviet Union no longer exists, we can still learn from its example.

The Soviet Union was born on November 7, 1917. Secretive and shadowy, it seldom revealed its inner workings. However, we, as astrologers, can look at its birth chart and discover the reasons for its actions. (See Chart No. 19.)

The U.S.S.R.
November 7, 1917

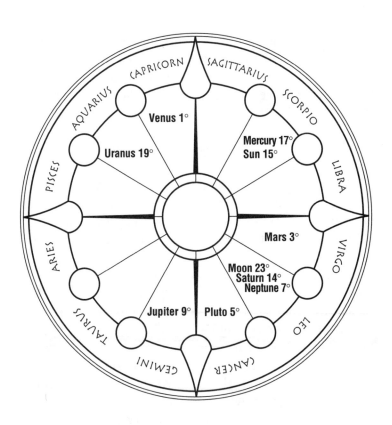

Chart No. 19

A look at the astrological aspects for November 7, 1917, reveals a very bad configuration. The Sun, Moon, Mercury, Saturn, Neptune, and Uranus are all arranged in a T-square formation, the worst aspect in astrology. Uranus, the planet of extremes, is badly aspected with Saturn, the planet of oppression. Saturn and Uranus are in opposition, a condition which astrologers Frances Sakoian and Louis Acker describe in their book *The Astrologer's Handbook* (Harper and Row, 1973) as follows:

"This opposition inclines the natives toward inconsistent and dictatorial attitudes. They will rarely practice what they preach. Their philosophy is idealistic, but their actions are oppressive. Desiring freedom for themselves, they are usually unwilling to grant it to others."

This is clearly a good description of the history of the Soviet Union.

Another aspect of interest in the chart of the Soviet Union is the square between Jupiter and Mars. This is an aspect for people who glorify war and waste resources on it: another accurate description of Soviet history.

All in all, the chart of the Soviet Union has eleven bad aspects and only five good aspects. This reflects the bad things that the Soviet government did when it existed, such as restricting the freedom of its own people and promoting communist dictatorships worldwide. Analysis of its chart supports the opinion that the Soviet Union was one of the most destructive political entities of the twentieth century.

The history of the twentieth century, however, shows the effects of transiting planets on the Soviet Union.

In the early 1960s Pluto and Uranus were in Virgo aligned in positive aspect with the Soviet Union's Sun and Mercury in Scorpio. During this time period, Nikita Khrushchev instituted a brief thaw in the internal restrictions in the Soviet Union. This period of relative freedom allowed authors like Aleksandr Solzhenitsyn to be published for the first time. Also during this time period, the Soviet Union was flying high in the space race, having beaten the United States into space by launching the Sputnik spacecraft.

In the late 1980s and early '90s, Pluto had moved into Scorpio, creating a dangerous situation for the Soviet Union. (See Chart No. 20.) Pluto is the planet of death and regeneration, and Scorpio is the sign of death and regeneration. The U.S.S.R. had reached a point where it had to regenerate or die.

I wrote an article for the January 1986 issue of *Venture Inward* magazine entitled, "Will Freedom Erupt in the Soviet Union?" In the article, I discussed the possible fall of the Soviet Union during this Pluto transit. Long before the Soviet Union fell, astrologer Liz Greene described this Pluto transit in her book *The Outer Planets and Their Cycles* (CRCS Publications, 1983):

> **What hasn't happened to Russia is the approaching transit of Pluto through Scorpio. The present political entity is too young to have experienced this transit before. I will be very curious indeed to see what comes of it. If Saturn brings down the head of the government, what will Pluto do? Perhaps the entire structure will change. Pluto always brings profound changes and rids a person of things which he has outgrown. It's a kind of fate. If the person can't meet the challenge to change, then he breaks down. That is very likely to happen in Russia, because there isn't a great deal of inclination shown to**

1991
Transiting T-Square for the U.S.S.R.

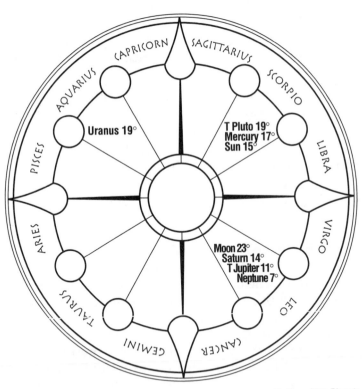

T = Transiting Planets

Chart No. 20

alter the system in any way except to tighten it . . .

You often see marriages breaking down when the outer planets transit over Venus. Russia is a conglomerate of many different nations, not all of which went into the marriage very willingly. Poland and Czechoslovakia and Hungary may be thinking of divorce . . .

Put simplistically, I would say that there will be a tremendous eruption from the collective, perhaps the beginnings of an internal revolution, happening at the same time that the central authority is not in a position to prevent it. Then there would be a period of disintegration, and a potential for a new birth . . .

The fact that Liz Greene was able to predict almost exactly what happened to the Soviet Union shows the amazing power of astrology, especially through the indications of outer planet transits. They affect nations as well as individuals.

The Astrology of the People's Republic of China

The People's Republic of China was born on October 1, 1949, in Beijing. A look at the planetary configuration on that date tells us a great deal about the past and future of China. (See Chart No. 21.)

Sun conjunct Neptune. This is an aspect for divine inspiration on the positive side and self-delusion on the negative side. Much depends on the transiting aspects to the conjunction at any given time. People with this aspect see life from their own point of view.

Mars conjunct Pluto. The planet of will is linked with the planet of anger in the chart of China. This can be a violent aspect because of the "do-or-die" attitude it conveys. During the Korean War, when transiting Pluto

People's Republic of China
October 1, 1949
Beijing

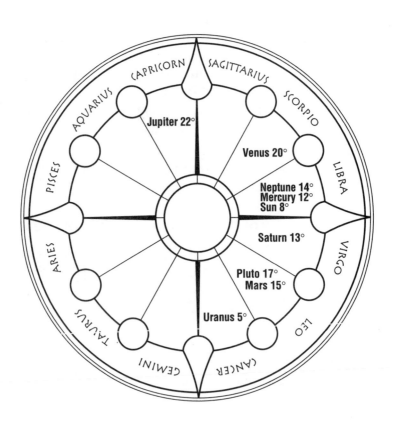

Chart No. 21

FREE CATALOG OF BOOKS AND MEMBERSHIP ACTIVITIES

Fill-in and mail this postage-paid card today.

Please write clearly

Name: _____

Address: _____

City: _____

State/Province: _____

Postal/Zip Code: _____ Country: _____

Association for Research and Enlightenment, Inc.
215 67th Street
Virginia Beach, VA 23451-2061

For Faster Service call 1-800-723-1112
www.are-cayce.com

was conjunct China's natal Mars, China almost overran the Korean peninsula by throwing human waves of troops at U.N. forces. Only a U.N. counterattack prevented it.

Sun square Uranus. This configuration indicates a tendency toward extreme egotism. People with this aspect can make vehement enemies. It is also present in the birth chart of the Soviet Union, another communist country. In a country's astrological chart, it can represent the tyranny of the government over the affairs of the people, as seems to be the case with communist systems.

Venus square Mars and Pluto. This configuration reflects the position of women in the People's Republic of China. Venus is the feminine, and women in China under the People's Republic have been very badly treated. There is, for example, a cultural prejudice against female babies. China has a higher percentage of male births to female births, and studies have shown that males are inherently more aggressive than females. A society with a disproportionate number of males, therefore, would be more aggressive as a society.

Sun-Mercury sextile Mars-Pluto. This is an aspect for tremendous energy and willpower. The aspect reflects the positive changes that occurred in China in the last quarter of the twentieth century. With enormous energy and drive, China transformed itself from a socialist agrarian economy to a capitalist industrial economy. After the death of Mao in the 1970s, Chairman Dung led China into the industrial age. The literacy rate was increased greatly, and the Chinese economy grew faster than any other economy in the world. The best thing the communist government did was give up on their communist economic system.

The Transiting Aspects for China

What is most interesting about the birth chart of the People's Republic of China is how the transiting planets over the last few years have reflected the recent history of China.

In the late 1970s, transiting Pluto moved into Libra and transiting Neptune moved into Sagittarius, aligning positively with China's natal Neptune, Mercury, and Sun in Libra as well as with its Pluto-Mars conjunction in Leo. This created aspects for regeneration and an explosive creative energy. The late '70s was the time period when Chairman Dung first began to reform the Chinese economy, and this led to its great expansion.

These good aspects continued until the outer planets had moved into a very negative configuration in June of 1989.

On June 5, 1989, the Chinese government ordered its troops to fire on peaceful prodemocracy demonstrators in Tiananmen Square in central Beijing. Hundreds of people were killed in this despicable act, and the transiting planets at that time show the violence of that moment.

On June 5, 1989, transiting Moon, Venus, and Mars were in Cancer; and transiting Saturn, Uranus, and Neptune were in Capricorn. This set up a powerful T-square in China's natal chart, involving a total of eleven natal and transiting planets. The transiting planets set off China's natal Sun square Uranus, an aspect for extremism. Also important was the fact that transiting Mars, the planet of violence, was in opposition to China's natal Jupiter. This is a very warlike aspect, and violence was the result.

The good news is that in the late twentieth and the early twenty-first century, the outer planets will line up in positive aspect with China's chart, possibly leading to a transformation not unlike the one the Soviet Union went through in the 1990s.

In the late '90s, transiting Pluto moves into Sagittarius and transiting Uranus and Neptune move into Aquarius, lining up in good aspect with China's natal Sun, Neptune, and Mercury in Libra. (See Chart No. 22.) These are aspects for an opening of awareness. There is a danger, however, because having transiting Uranus-Neptune in Aquarius creates an opposition with China's natal Mars-Pluto in Leo, so there is the possibility of violence.

Edgar Cayce had several interesting things to say about China's future in his readings that seem to fit these diverse aspects:

> **If there is not the acceptance in America of the closer brotherhood of man, the love of neighbor as self, civilization must wend its way westward— and again must Mongolia, must a hated people, be raised.** 3976-15

A concept that is brought up several times in the Cayce readings is that civilization is continuously moving westward. For example, first came the Roman Empire, then the British Empire, and today we have the American Empire, each farther west than the preceding. Cayce tells us that if the United States does not live up to its obligations with respect to the love of its neighbors and all humankind, then civilization will begin to move westward, once again indicating a possible reemergance of China as a major world power.

Cayce's prophecy matches the transiting Uranus-Neptune natal Mars-Pluto opposition discussed earlier. Contrast that with the following reading that seems to match the positive "opening of awareness" aspects for China:

2000
Transiting Sextiles for the
People's Republic of China

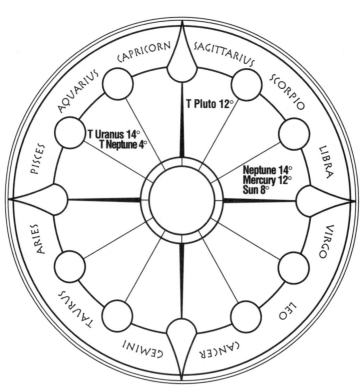

T Pluto 12°

T Uranus 14°
T Neptune 4°

Neptune 14°
Mercury 12°
Sun 8°

T = Transiting Planets

Chart No. 22

The sin of China? Yea, there is the quietude that will not be turned aside, saving itself by the slow growth. There has been a growth, a stream through the land in ages which asks to be left alone to be just satisfied with that within itself. It awoke one day and cut its hair off! And it began to think and to do something with its thinking! This, here, will be one day the cradle of Christianity, as applied in the lives of men. Yea, it is far off as man counts time, but only a day in the heart of God—for tomorrow China will awake. Let each and every soul as they come to those understandings, do something, then, in his or her own heart.   3976-29

Cayce says that one day China will be "the cradle of Christianity." This transformation could come during the favorable outer-planet aspects of the late twentieth and the early twenty-first centuries.

9

THE ASTROLOGY OF WORLD EVENTS

Not only do transiting astrological aspects affect individuals, they affect the world as well. When negative astrological aspects occur, challenges are presented on the earth. When positive astrological aspects occur, we have times of peace and prosperity on the earth. Astrological aspects affect world events. This chapter will explore how the planets influenced events on earth during various time periods.

In April of 1941, Edgar Cayce gave several readings in which he said that the astrological aspects at the time were very unusual. In the following, Gertrude Cayce, Edgar Cayce's wife, conducted the reading:

> *Mrs. Cayce: In the light of the information given through this channel this morning, April 28, 1941, regarding astrological aspects for the next two weeks, and our desire to use this for the good of all, you will please advise us as to the character of changes to take place and how we may constructively meet them. You will then answer the questions, as I ask them.*

Mr. Cayce: Yes, we have the information that has been indicated through these channels regarding astrological influences and their effect upon the future thought of each soul now manifesting in the earth.

As is understood by many, in the earth manifestation and the cycle of time much repeats itself; and those in authority, in high and low places, have the opportunity for individual expression—that wields an influence upon those who are directed in body, mind or thought or spirit by the activities of those manifesting in the earth.

As to those experiences paralleling the cycle of astrological activity now—beginning on the morrow—there will be the Sun, the Moon, Jupiter, Uranus and Venus all in the one sign.

When last this occurred, as indicated, the earth throughout was in turmoil, in strife.

There are still influences indicated in the lives of groups banded as nations, banded as peoples, still influenced by those happenings.

What then, ye ask, is the influence that makes for this great change that may be expected?

The powers of light and darkness, as then, as sixteen hundred (1600) years before. As in those periods, so today—we find nation against nation; the powers of death, destruction, the wrecking of that which has been and is held near and dear to the hearts of those who have through one form or another set ideals.   3976-26

From astrological aspects every soul in the earth, in the present experience, will think differently, will have varied urges from the happenings as will come to pass in the next two weeks. Not merely because of the unusual astrological aspects, but more because each entity through

its awareness in physical consciousness, in cosmic consciousness, has come in the environ of the ruling forces of the astrological aspects that are to be so active in the affairs of man in his relationships one to another during this period—from April the 29th to May the 12th, 1941. It has been over eight hundred years since such has been the urge. Think of the darkness of the spiritual life as was enacted then, and see what is the experience through which so many souls are passing and will pass during this period in the relationships of man to man.   2550-1

The readings tell us that it had been hundreds of years since the astrological influences were as unusual as they were in the spring of 1941. He said that it was a time when the forces of light and darkness were battling on the earth. These influences can be easily seen by looking at the astrological aspects for May 10, 1941. (See Chart No. 23.)

On that day there was a conjunction of the Sun, Mercury, Venus, Jupiter, Saturn, and Uranus in the sign of Taurus. These planets were all in a bad aspect with Mars and the Moon. The arrangement was the familiar T-square, the worst configuration in astrology.

What is interesting about this grouping is that all the planets are square Mars, the planet of war, violence, and aggression: Sun square Mars, Moon square Mars, Mercury square Mars, Jupiter square Mars, Saturn square Mars, and Uranus square Mars. It does not get any worse than this with regard to war and violence.

May 10, 1941, was the date of the worst bombing raid on London during all of World War II. The Germans dropped incendiary bombs, which the winds whipped into a firestorm that destroyed 10,000 buildings and killed thousands of people.

The Bombing of London
May 10, 1941

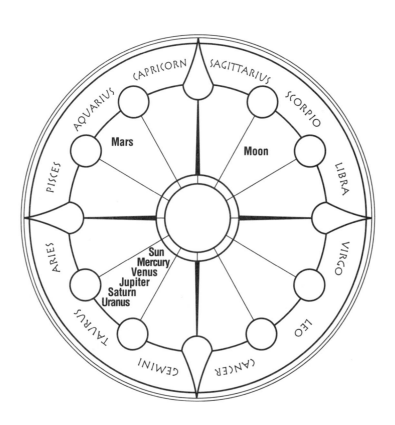

Chart No. 23

If one looks at what was going on in the world on that day, one could almost say it was the lowest point of civilization for the twentieth century. Stalin was in power in Russia, Tojo in Japan, and Hitler in Germany. The Germans had conquered most of Europe, and England was fighting alone against Hitler. This was all reflected in the astrological aspects of that time and day.

The Astrology of D-Day

A few years later, on June 6, 1944, the planets had shifted into a very positive configuration. It was the date of D-Day, the Allied invasion of Europe. (See Chart No. 24.)

A look at the astrological chart for that date shows that eight of the ten planets were arranged in positive aspect with each other.

The events of the time reflect these positive aspects. The Normandy invasion was carried out by many thousands of brave men willing to sacrifice themselves to free the continent of Europe from Nazi tyranny, and this bravery is shown in the astrological aspects.

Pluto, the planet of will, is conjunct Mars, the planet of action. Pluto and Mars together represent a "do-or-die" type of energy. What could constitute more of a "do-or-die" situation than landing on the Normandy beaches?

Another reflection of these positive astrological aspects was the outcome of the invasion: It was ultimately successful, largely because of its auspicious beginning.

Not only did these aspects work on a general level, but for General Dwight D. Eisenhower as well.

General Eisenhower, the commander of the Normandy invasion, was a Libra. On June 6, 1944, the Sun, Venus, Mars, Jupiter, Saturn, Uranus, and Pluto were all lined

D-Day
June 6, 1944

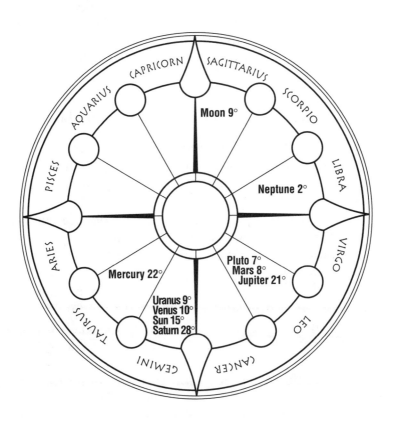

Chart No. 24

up in positive aspect with the sign of Libra. When so many outer planets are lined up with a person's natal Sun position, it represents a time of destiny in his or her life. In fact, in examining Eisenhower's life, one could easily surmise that the decision to launch the invasion was the defining moment of his life.

The story is familiar—the weather was bad, and there was some question as to whether to go ahead with the invasion. Eisenhower took a walk alone on the beach to make the decision. He decided to go ahead, and the decision turned out to have been the correct one.

So the aspects were good for the world and for Eisenhower as well.

The Astrology of the Hiroshima Bombing

An extraordinary moment in history, such as the dropping of the atomic bomb on Hiroshima, should be reflected in the astrological aspects for that time and date, and they are.

This event is interesting from an astrological viewpoint because we know the exact day, time, and place in which it occurred. This allows us to draw an exact astrological chart.

The Hiroshima bomb exploded at 8:16 a.m., August 6, 1945. The astrological aspects for that time and place mirror the violent nature of the event, especially if you use Cayce's way of judging astrology. (See Chart No. 25.)

Cayce said that in addition to being indicators of planetary sojourns, the most influential planets in an astrological chart were the Sun and the planets closest to the ascendant and the midheaven. When the Hiroshima bomb exploded, Mars, the planet of war and violence, was on the midheaven. In addition, Uranus,

The Bombing of Hiroshima
August 6, 1945
8:16 a.m.

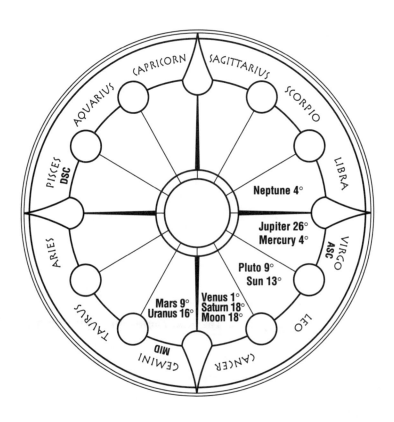

Chart No. 25

the planet of extremes, was close to the midheaven and in the same sign as Mars. The Hiroshima bomb reflected the most extreme weapon that had ever been used.

On August 6, 1945, the Sun was conjunct Pluto, the planet of atomic energy. The atomic bomb harnessed the power of the sun by splitting the atom.

Pluto, also the planet of death and regeneration, was sextile Mars, the planet of war. This aspect shows the determination of the Americans to end the war by using the atom bomb—and end it they did.

The aspects for August 6, 1945, show the dual nature of the event: a terrible destruction for the city of Hiroshima, but a blessing in the sense that it, along with the bombing of Nagasaki two days later, ended a terrible war once and for all.

The Astrology of the Summer of Love

One day I was watching a TV special on the music of the 1960s. A number of musicians were talking about the concerts they had played in California in the summer of 1967, and they mentioned how there were "special vibrations" that summer; that they had felt these vibrations during their concerts. That feeling and the events that followed were so powerful that the press called it "the summer of love."

The summer of love marked the height of the counterculture movement of the 1960s. The positive aspects of the flower children and the openness and freedom of expression were felt by all.

On hearing these musicians discuss the positive vibrations of that summer, I was struck by the sincerity of their feelings about the love they felt was in the air at the time. It intrigued me, and, as an astrologer, I immediately went to my ephemeris to see how the astrological aspects that summer indicated that it was indeed a summer of love.

The first astrological aspects to explore are aspects to Venus, the planet of love. As one might expect, in the summer of 1967 there were very positive aspects to Venus almost all summer. (See Chart No. 26.)

Beginning in June 1967, Venus and Jupiter were conjunct in Leo. These are the two most benevolent planets in astrology. Venus, the planet of love and beauty, and Jupiter, the planet of the masses and universal consciousness, were together in the powerful sign of Leo.

This Venus-Jupiter conjunction was trine Saturn in Aries. The two largest planets, Jupiter and Saturn, trine each other with Venus, the goddess of love, added to the mix. No wonder people felt special vibrations during the summer of 1967!

After the June configuration, Venus moved into Virgo in July, and then in August was aligned in positive aspect with Mars in Scorpio. Any Venus-Mars link is an aspect for the balance of male and female energies. This created more positive love energy for the summer of love.

By September 1967 Venus had, by retrograde motion, moved back into Leo and was conjunct Jupiter again. Almost the entire summer, from June till September, Venus was in and out of positive aspect with a number of planets, and these aspects helped create that special vibration of love that people felt that summer.

The Astrology of the *Challenger* Explosion

In January of 1986, the United States space shuttle *Challenger* exploded shortly after takeoff. Faulty "O rings" on the solid rocket booster had burned through and set off a tank of liquid hydrogen destroying the

The Summer of Love
July 1, 1967

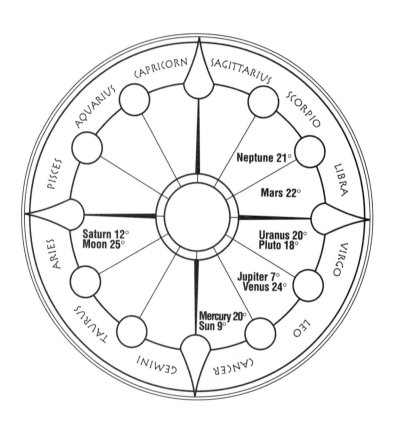

Neptune 21°

Mars 22°

Saturn 12°
Moon 25°

Uranus 20°
Pluto 18°

Jupiter 7°
Venus 24°

Mercury 20°
Sun 9°

Chart No. 26

spacecraft and killing the crew. It was the worst tragedy in the history of the United States space program.

The cause of the O-ring failure was related to the extremely cold weather conditions on the day of the launch. There were literally icicles hanging off the *Challenger* before it was launched. Engineers felt that the cold may have caused the O rings to malfunction.

When the *Challenger* exploded, I checked the planetary positions for that day to see if they showed any indication that a disaster would take place.

The astrological aspects for 11:38 a.m., January 28, 1986, do indicate the possibility of explosive conditions. (See Chart No. 27.) The most striking aspect was Mars square Jupiter. Mars, the most explosive, violent, planet, was in bad aspect with Jupiter, the expansive planet; or, to put it another way, Jupiter, big, and Mars, explosive, leads to a big explosion. This is exactly the kind of aspect you would expect to see for this kind of event.

Any sort of Mars square could apply, including Mars square Uranus, Mars square Saturn, or Mars square Neptune.

The Mars-square-Jupiter aspect also matches the human conditions surrounding the accident. Some engineers had warned NASA management that the O rings might fail and that their structural integrity should be reexamined. NASA management ignored these warnings and went ahead with the launch anyway. This aggressive attitude on the part of NASA management is reflective of the Mars-square-Jupiter aspect. It is a decidedly masculine aspect, and the vast majority of NASA managers are men. In this case, they acted in an overly aggressive manner reflective of a Mars square.

Another series of aspects was the Sun, Venus, and Mercury all being square to Pluto, the planet of death and regeneration. These are also aspects for willfulness

The *Challenger* Explosion
January 28, 1986
11:38 a.m.

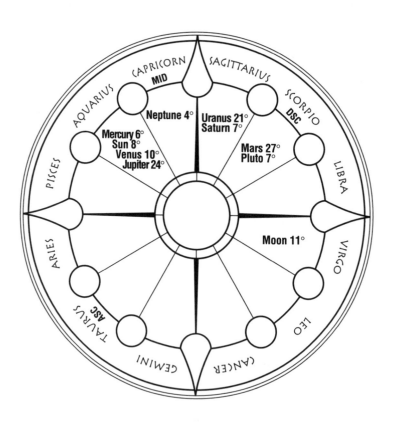

Chart No. 27

and dictatorial attitudes. NASA had a launch schedule they were determined to keep, and this sense of pressure to keep the schedule is shown in the Pluto aspects and may have contributed to the disaster.

The Astrology of Waco

On April 19, 1993, FBI and ATF agents raided the compound of the Branch Davidian sect in Waco, Texas. As the federal agents moved in, sect members spread lantern fuel all over the compound and set it on fire. Most of the sect members perished in the fire.

The astrological aspects for that day show some of the starkest evidence for a relationship between astrology and the deeds of humankind. (See Chart No. 28.)

The astrological aspects for April 19, 1993, were extremely bad. Uranus and Neptune were conjunct in Capricorn, and square the Sun in Aries. This is an aspect for religious self-delusion. The Branch Davidian sect, led by the self-proclaimed prophet David Koresh, believed that the end of the world was near and that the world would be destroyed in a fiery conflagration. This became a self-fulfilling prophecy as the compound was set on fire and burned to the ground.

Not only was the Sun square the Uranus-Neptune conjunction on that day, but the Sun was also square Mars, the planet of violence. This set up a T-square involving religious self-delusion and violence. This fits the situation, since the religious cult had exchanged gunfire with federal authorities before setting the compound on fire. A T-square with the Sun, Mars, Uranus, and Neptune is about as bad as it gets.

These Mars aspects also apply to the federal agents in that Mars in bad aspect tends to make people overly aggressive. The government attacked the compound,

Waco, Texas
April 19, 1993

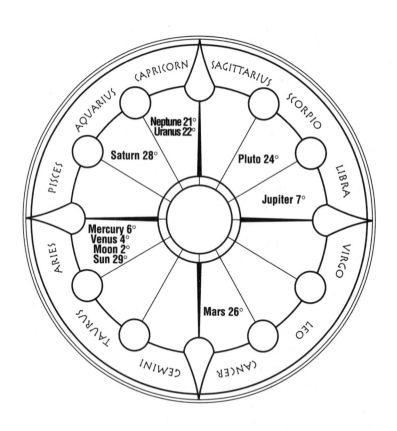

Chart No. 28

not knowing that the result would be so terrible. Most people believe that it would have been better if they had waited and tried longer to resolve the standoff peacefully.

In addition to the Mars aspects on April 19, Saturn, the lord of karma, was square Pluto, the planet of death and regeneration. As I have mentioned before, any Pluto aspect can produce dictatorial tendencies, and this can lead to a confrontation like we saw at Waco.

Finally, the Moon, Venus, and Mercury were in opposition to Jupiter on the day of the raid. How remarkable that all ten of the planets were in bad aspect on that day! No wonder the result of the raid was so terrible.

One thing that the raid on the Branch Davidian compound shows us is how valuable astrology can be. If the government agents had been familiar with astrology, they would have never picked April 19 to raid the compound. They would have waited another month until the aspects were more favorable, and perhaps events would have turned out much better.

The Astrology of the Billy Graham Broadcast

The last event to consider astrologically is the worldwide Billy Graham television broadcast of March 18, 1995. On that day, the Christian minister, Billy Graham, broadcast his message of Christ to 150 countries around the world. The broadcast was translated into 180 different languages, and it is estimated that the total audience was 500 million people. It was a great feat, bringing Jesus' message of love and peace to people in vast numbers all over the earth. It was an event that in many ways was the opposite of the violent events we have examined. The astrological aspects for that date reflect the extremely positive nature of the broadcast. (See Chart No. 29.)

On March 18, 1995, the Sun was aligned in positive aspect with the three outer planets, Uranus, Neptune, and Pluto. I have emphasized in this book that when the outer planets are aligned in positive aspect with the Sun, it represents a time of destiny. For a television minister such as Billy Graham, such a worldwide broadcast was a life achievement.

Sun sextile Uranus-Neptune and trine Pluto has all the elements for such an occasion. Neptune is the mystic, Uranus rules television and the electronic media, and Pluto rules the masses. So the broadcast involved bringing a mystical message to the masses through television. It also matches Dr. Graham's personal astrology, since he is a Scorpio, and his natal Sun position would match up well with Uranus and Neptune in Capricorn, and the Sun, Saturn, and Mercury in Pisces.

Positive events like the Billy Graham broadcast are generally more difficult to evaluate than negative events because negative events tend to be more dramatic, and the media tends to focus more on them. However, over the years I have noticed that peace negotiations between disputing sides tend to move forward when these positive outer planet aspects are in effect. But the moving forward of peace negotiations is not usually recognized as a big flashy event. Nonetheless, one can see these positive trends when positive aspects are in place.

An interesting example of both sides of these kinds of aspects came during the Persian Gulf War. In July 1990, there were some very bad Mars aspects, and Saddam Hussein massed his troops on the border of Kuwait, invading it in early August. Five months later, on January 16, 1991, coalition forces attacked Iraq with air raids. The aspects for January 16, 1991, were extremely good, and the coalition forces did not lose a single plane during the attack. Good aspects bring good results.

Billy Graham Broadcast
March 18, 1995

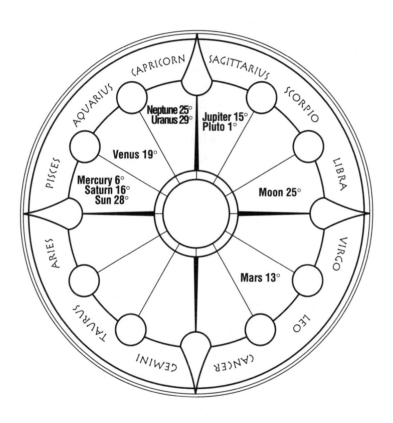

Neptune 25°
Uranus 29°

Jupiter 15°
Pluto 1°

Venus 19°

Mercury 6°
Saturn 16°
Sun 28°

Moon 25°

Mars 13°

CAPRICORN
SAGITTARIUS
AQUARIUS
SCORPIO
PISCES
LIBRA
ARIES
VIRGO
TAURUS
LEO
GEMINI
CANCER

Chart No. 29

The Age of Aquarius

In this book we have looked at personal astrology, but another important astrological reality now occurring is that we are moving from the Age of Pisces to the Age of Aquarius. Because of the relative movement of the earth with respect to the background stars, every 2,165 years we move from one astrological age to the next.

One fascinating thing about this is that every time the astrological age changes, our religious symbols also change. During the previous age, the Age of Aries— 2165 B.C. to 165 B.C., the religious symbols revolved around the sign of Aries, a fire sign symbolized by the ram. The religious rituals then used involved sacrificing rams on an altar of fire. This took place in Jewish worship and is discussed at length in the Old Testament. Other religious fire symbols during that time included use of the temple menorah, a candlestand whose candles were kept burning constantly by attending priests.

The Age of Aries ended when the Temple was desecrated by a Syrian king, Antiocus Epiphanes, in 165 B.C.

The present age, the Age of Pisces, which began in 165 B.C., has religious symbols that revolve around the sign of Pisces, a water sign symbolized by the fish. Jesus was the physical embodiment of the Piscean Age. He walked on water, calmed the water, was baptized in water, turned water into wine, multiplied the fishes and the loaves, and called the fish into the nets; He was even called the "fisher of men." People today even use the Greek word for fish, *ichthys*, as a symbol for Jesus.

In addition, Pisces is the martyr's sign, and the Piscean Age began with the martyrdom of Jesus.

The next age, the Age of Aquarius, will have religious

symbols revolving around the sign of Aquarius, an air sign symbolized by a man carrying a pitcher of water. Edgar Cayce predicted that the Age of Aquarius would be the age of electronics:

> **As we would give, as we shall see from the application of the entity in and through earthly sojourns, the entity should begin now to study electronics. For as the earth and the peoples of same enter Aquarius, the air, we find that the electrical forces, electronics and energies are to be the ruling influences—by the very position of same in the spheres of the system which the earth occupies merely as a space or place in the present.** 3902-2

Cayce also said that the Age of Aquarius would be an age when the world would be united in universal fellowship and that there would be a thousand years of peace on the earth. Let us hope that Cayce is right and that Aquarius leads us to that wonderful future.

It is clear from this study of Edgar Cayce's view of astrology that astrology influences world events in the extreme. When large groupings of planets are in particular aspects, it affects the world in different ways. These influences are many and varied and do not enable us to make specific predictions, but we can glimpse the general tenor of events to come. For example, when there are negative Mars aspects, wars tend to break out. When aspects are positive, peace talks and peace agreements become the order of the day.

But the Cayce readings show that the human will is superior to any astrological influences. How this works on an individual level can best be illustrated by the story of a friend of mine named Bill.

Bill asked me to do his astrological chart, and, in

looking at it, I was surprised to find that his soul took its flight to earth from Saturn, the planet of disappointment and change. When I asked Bill about this, he told me that he had suffered from depression for many years and at one point was so low that he even considered suicide. This is what one would expect from a Saturn sojourn.

But then one day Bill had a vision of the Virgin Mary. She came to him and showed him the earth from outer space. On the earth were many bright points of light. Mary pointed to one of the points of light and said to him, "That's you!" After this vision Bill never suffered from depression again because he realized his place in the universe as a bright point of light.

A person can come into this life with one influence from the past, but we can change! Cayce's past lives show this very well. In one life he comes from Jupiter; in another from Uranus; and in another from Arcturus. We ourselves are the main influence. We are the power. We can choose any astrological influence we wish. That is the beauty of the human will.

So, astrology has an influence, but, as Bill's story shows, what is most important is that we remember that we are in control of our lives and we all are bright points of light.

Martin Crespo
305 — 259 — 84 44

786 — 443 — 5656

DISCOVER HOW THE EDGAR CAYCE MATERIAL CAN HELP YOU!

The Association for Research and Enlightenment, Inc. (A.R.E.®), was founded in 1931 by Edgar Cayce. Its international headquarters are in Virginia Beach, Virginia, where thousands of visitors come year-round. Many more are helped and inspired by A.R.E.'s local activities in their own hometowns or by contact via mail (and now the Internet!) with A.R.E. headquarters.

People from all walks of life, all around the world, have discovered meaningful and life-transforming insights in the A.R.E. programs and materials, which focus on such areas as holistic health, dreams, family life, finding your best vocation, reincarnation, ESP, meditation, personal spirituality, and soul growth in small-group settings. Call us today on our toll-free number:

1-800-333-4499

or

Explore our electronic visitor's center on the
INTERNET: http://www.edgarcayce.org

We'll be happy to tell you more about how the work of the A.R.E. can help you!

A.R.E.
215 67th Street
Virginia Beach, VA 23451-2061